A
Long Way
From
Pollard

by

Gwendolyn Comley Lentz

Copyright © 2013 by Gwendolyn Comley Lentz

All rights reserved. This book or any portion thereof may not be reproduced or used in any manner whatsoever without the express written permission of the publisher except for the use of brief quotations in a book review.

ISBN 978-1-304-37309-0

Printed in the United States of America

First Printing, 2013

The author may be contacted at:

3674 Marlborough Way
Paducah, KY 42001

This book is dedicated to my brother, Victor Comley, my youngest daughter, Carol Ann Keeling and to my husband Bill Lentz. Without Victor's endless supply of stories and memories, I could never have written anything worth reading. (Or is it?) Also, had Carol Ann not nagged me to write "all these old stories down" I would never have undertaken such a task. And to Bill, who helped in more ways than one. First, he has never complained about the inflated monthly telephone bill when I would be right in the middle of some story and couldn't read my own hastily scribbled notes and would be forced to call Vic for clarification. Secondly, when he realized that I was becoming serious about this endeavor, he suggested that I buy a computer to make life a little easier.

Gwen Comley Lentz, Age 6

Editors note

This book was written over a period of twenty years. During that time life continued apace with births, deaths, marriages, celebrations and misfortunes. This book has not been updated to take those events into account – it is presented as it was written. Gwen notes that "These stories are a mixture of fact, fiction and legend. Some Pollardites no doubt remember things differently – these are my memories and my Pollard."

The author is indebted to Robin Fain who served as Editor of the 1993 book History of Jessamine County, Kentucky, published by the Jessamine County Historical and Genealogical Society, Inc. Robin generously allowed the use of certain historical information in that book.

Table of Contents

Early Life 1
Reynolds's Store 19
Mother's Diaries 30
That Ol' Time Religion 33
Readin' Writin' and 'Rithmatic.................................. 43
Hog Killin', Cannin' and Preservin' 53
Grandpa and Mommy Johns 56
Uncle Clay and Aunt Laura 73
Aunt Vina and Uncle Harry 77
Uncle Roland 85
Uncle Homer and Aunt Hazel 90
Uncle Herbert and Aunt Mayme 93
Uncle Elmer and Aunt Dallas.................................... 98
Pollard and Some of Its Residents........................... 101
Sickness, Death and Funerals 112
Amusements and Entertainment 123
Earning Money 129
Granny and Grandad's House 132
Great Grandma House 140
Superstitions, Signs and Omens 145
High School 148
The War Years 160
Sex Education in the Thirties.................................. 172
Great Aunts and Uncles 174
Mother and Daddy 180

Epilogue   *190*

Early Life

Okay, Carol Ann, I've heard that refrain long enough. Namely, "Mother, you've got to write all those old stories down. You know we'll never remember them if you don't." Of course I can't understand why because I tell them every time more than one member of the family comes near. Maybe that's why she wants it written down, and then she won't have to listen to the one about Uncle Homer and the Donaldson Bread man during every Christmas dinner. Now it is not my intent to ramble on about the good ol' days. I'll tell you the stories and what life was like when I was a child and you can decide for yourself. And besides, if I don't do this, how will you and your children and your children's children know who their people were and what Pollard was like before the roads were paved, and electricity and running water made life easier.

Late in the day of April 23, 1926, a 24 year old woman lay on a feather bed in the home of her mother and father, Cordie and Will Johns. Her name was Dola Johns Comley and she had just given birth to her second child. Sometime later, Will walked in, looked at the baby and said, "Well, what have you done?" She replied, "I've just done the hardest days work I have ever done in my life."

I was born at the home of my Grandparents. They lived in the small community of Pollard, which is located in Jessamine County, Kentucky. These were my mother's parents and their names were Will and Cordelia (Cordie) Johns. We called them "Mommy and Grandpa Johns." My other Grandparents lived across the road. They were Owen and Laura (Laurey) Comley. We called them "Granny and Grandad."

Ocie Butler and Gwendolyn Comley, August 21, 1926

The immediate family consisted of mother (Dola), father (Calvin), and Victor and me. Victor is 6 years older than I. In today's society, Granny and Grandad would be called our extended family. No one could have convinced us that they were not our immediate family. Dad was their only child; therefore we were the only grandchildren. We considered everything they owned to be ours also. When I spoke of our house, I meant Granny and Grandad's house. When I described rose bushes in our front yard, it was their front yard to which I referred. That was the Home Place, and all the other places we lived were just that; a place to live. We stayed with them more than we did our parents. We were theirs and they were ours.

Grandad was a kind and gentle man with a wry sense of humor. He almost always had the beginning of a smile on his face but he was also cursed with a feisty streak. Once, back in the early twenties he agreed to bring one of the Lexington Rosenberg's a bushel of walnuts for a quarter. They owned a store with a main street location. Merchandise lined each wall but the shiny marble floor was uncluttered by display tables. When Grandad brought the walnuts (which for some reason he called warnets) and expected to receive his payment, Mr. Rosenberg informed him that he had changed his mind. Grandad calmly picked up the basket and with one forward motion flung them down that marble hall and walked out. He later reported with some satisfaction, that "warnets" went everywhere.

There were more land disputes over line fences than any other subject. With perhaps the exception of some woman. Grandad and Wolford Miller "fell out" over a line fence on the Bill Ev Hillside. (Hillsides and pastures all had names.) They had a disagreement and Wolford shot at Grandad. Fortunately, the bullet hit a fence post instead and Grandad hauled him into court. He was fined $500.00, and they didn't speak for years. Grandad made the first attempt at reconciliation by saying, "We're both getting old, why don't we shake hands and put all this behind us?" The response was, "Well, will you get me back my $500.00?" Grandad said, "Ay, I wouldn't give ye hay if ye was a mule." And that was the last time either spoke to the other. Grandad had a wonderful sense of humor. Once, in reference to a particularly awkward Pollard resident, who borrowed neighbors' tools, he said, "He's tore up everything but a crowbar and he bent that." At the age of eighteen, he was thrown from a horse resulting in an injury to his hip, which required a lifelong means of assistance in mobility. Since this was in the days before hip replacements and the aluminum walker, he always relied upon the aid of a broomstick, which he carried in his right hand and used instead of a cane. In his later years, he needed one in both hands. I can still hear the sounds he made while walking through the house. As one broomstick hit the floor, one foot slowly shuffled forward then the other stick moved forward. In height, he was probably a bit less than five feet tall and while he was not at all fat, he was thick set. But someone said he was the gamest (bravest) little man he had ever known. As he aged, he became almost bald with the exception of a ring of snow-white hair around his head.

He was a very hard worker at any job that he was physically able to do, but many times Victor and I were called on for little tasks that were beyond his ability, and since Vic was six years older than I, he stayed with them far more than I did. And did a lot more work than I ever thought of doing. Well, I was often called upon to draw a bucket of water, and that didn't mean get some paper and a box of colors. It meant go to the cistern, hang a granite bucket over the spout and turn the handle until the water came gushing up. When filled, it was carried to the back porch or kitchen.

Every year, one of us had to help Grandad plant his beloved "daihliards." Grandad's brother, Henry, lived in Irvine, Kentucky. Uncle Henry's occupation was Dentistry and in his spare time, grew prize-winning dahlias, which he generously shared with Grandad. After he had dug the hole, shovel in one hand, broomstick in the other, it was my job to get down on hands and knees and place the bulbs just so. They grew so tall that they always had to be staked to prevent their falling over. Some varieties had flowers as large as saucers.

He had a great propensity for the mispronunciation of words. Once when we went to Wilmore to Big Camp Meeting, Granny packed a big basket of food. This was known as Dinner on the Ground. She had fried two or three chickens, made potato salad, sliced tomatoes, corn and green beans and as she unrolled a quilt, and spread everything about, she noticed we had neighbors who were also preparing their dinner. They saw our fried chicken, mentioned they had brought Belgium Hare and wondered if a trade would be possible. Granny was always so nosy; she had to try everything so she gave them some chicken and they gave us some Belgium Hare. Grandad took one bite, threw it on the ground and said, "Ay, I can't go no Belgimum Hare."

One of Uncle Ira's daughters was named Ima Jeannette. Grandad turned that one into Jumanet.

Another job for Grandad and me was spring painting. He painted the window frames while I painted the woodwork and varnished any floors that weren't covered by linoleum "carpets." I learned to paint and varnish at an early age. I remember one summer I had to paint the entire floor of the front porch. I really enjoyed painting, for it was a grown up job. I seldom had to do any such chores at any of the other houses but always had work to do for them. I carried water from the cistern, brought in wood and coal, gathered eggs and always had to go to some far pasture to bring the cows to the barn lot. There were three or four cows. One cow wore a bell around her neck. If I could get behind her and head her in the direction of the barn, then I had it made. The others followed that bell.

As soon as I was big enough, I learned to milk. That was a job I hated. I didn't like walking in the barn lot, especially after a heavy rain. In fact, there wasn't much I did like about cows with the exception of squirting milk in a city cousin's face. When our Irvine cousins came to visit we asked them if they wanted to see where the milk came from. We got our milking stools, put the bucket under the cow's bag, and aimed her teat right at the cousin's face. Then, urging a closer inspection to get a better view of the hole, we'd give a quick squeeze and he'd get a faceful. We could only do that one time though. We patted the cow on the right hip, said, "Saw heifer." And she moved her right leg back like a good heifer should. We also had barnyard cats and it was fun to tease them into standing on their hind legs while we squirted milk in their mouths. ("Gwen - quit wasting the milk!")

After the cows were stripped of all the milk, it was carried to the house, strained and run through the separator; an apparatus used for separating the milk from the cream. We also churned our own butter. The cream was put in a glass or wooden churn. The wooden churn sat on the floor and we filled it with cream, inserted the dasher, and covered with the wooden lid. Then came the hard part. The dasher was pulled up, pushed down, pulled up, pushed down. Granny could almost make the churn walk. Finally the butter would separate from the milk; this was called gather, because it gathered together. She then lifted it from the churn and shaped into molds with a wooden butter paddle.

They would have had a stroke at the thought of eating margarine instead of butter or toast for breakfast rather than hot biscuits. Along about 1931, Ford Motor Company opened a plant in Dayton, Ohio. Mother and Daddy left Victor and me with Grandad and Granny and moved to Dayton, renting a small upstairs apartment. The Company paid a going wage of five dollars a day and that was much better than a dollar or dollar and a half for setting tobacco in Pollard. Grandad hired someone to take him and Victor for a short visit. Mother got breakfast (that's what we said instead of cooked breakfast) and since she didn't have butter, served margarine. Well, Grandad took one bite and as was his custom when something didn't suit his taste, said "Ay, I can't go that."

Occasionally in the spring, cows would wander into a pasture replete with wild onions. Of course this filtered through the digestive system, the blood stream, and into the milk. Nothing was as disgusting as onion flavored milk. Most of us switched to iced tea or water until they were killed by summer heat. Almost as bad was blinky milk; which was the stage it reached just before it turned into clabber resembling cooked custard, except it was white. Mother cooked clabber and made wonderful homemade cottage cheese. (I didn't like it, but everyone else did.) Milk was never pasteurized or homogenized. And I never knew of anyone having a problem.

The cows all had names, but I only remember the name of one. She was "Ol' Node."

Granny and Grandad had a horse and buggy. The horse's name was Ol' Mae. The buggy was black as the ace of spades; I never saw a buggy of another color. They were a more comfortable means of travel than a wagon. Wagons were meant to haul tobacco, corn and lumber. Buggies were for the purpose of transporting people. They were light and airy; the seat was balanced on springs that made for a comfortable little outing although they did have a few inconveniences. Getting caught in a sudden rainstorm with the wind blowing in your face was one; another was sitting directly behind a gassy horse that had no manners. Nevertheless, Granny would hitch Ol' Mae to the buggy and off we went to spend the day with Aunt Doney, or Aunt Lizzie Peel or Aunt Minnie Lee Cooley. These were all great aunts. In Pollard, we didn't say aunts or ahants, we said "aints." We also said "daynce" for dance, "cain't" for can't' "arn" for iron, "dubye" for the letter W, "chimley" for chimney. We didn't wash clothes we warshed them and then we rinched them.

We didn't have mirrors, we had looking glasses. There were many others; if we had pronounced these words correctly, we would have been laughed at for trying to "talk proper" or "gittin above yer raisin." Once, Aunt Vina brought one of her grandchildren to Pollard to visit Mommy Johns. Her name was Dee Ann and she had never heard anything like a Pollard accent. She laughed and told Aunt Vina that "Granny had told her to raise the winder."

The "a" at the end of a given name was transformed into a "y" (or sometimes "ie'.) Aint Ida was Aint Idy, Vina was Viney, Laura was Laurey, Cordelia was Cordie and one of my schoolmates, Elizabeth Reynolds, was Lizzybeth. Gleama Stinnett was Gleamy. Gleamy was the only child we knew who was adopted and she also picked up a dynamite cap that blew off most of the fingers on that hand.

We never had a headache, we had the headache. When cancer was spoken of at all, it was "a cancer." We were forever "fixin" to do this or that or we might "get around to it dreckly."

My accent has gone through several changes during the years, but if I take a trip to another section of the country, that Pollard twang comes back so strong that even ah don no whut ah'm sayin muhsayuf.

Both of my grandmothers wore their hair combed straight back, twisted around, then coiled into a "bun" or a "biscuit" that rested on top of or at the back of the head. It was held tight by strategically placed hairpins or a small curved comb. I can never remember a woman of that age wearing her hair in any other style.

If they knew they would be exposed to the sun for any length of time, they always wore a cotton bonnet. These were handmade and usually decorated with rickrack or lace. Or both, depending on the artistry of the seamstress. They always had a ruffle in back for the purpose of shielding the neck from the summer sun. They wore aprons to keep their dresses clean. They wore an overall type apron, which opened in back and tied at the waist. I could never understand why Mommy Johns wore an apron. She much preferred fieldwork to housework and most of the time her "print" dresses were as dirty as her aprons. With the promise of an egg or two she could talk Esther and me into helping her plant beans in Uncle Elmer's corn patch. She sewed pockets on all her clothes. Her dresses, aprons, petticoats, and even her cotton "drawers" had pockets. When we were in that hot cornfield and saw all those pockets filled with beans to plant, we soon lost our enthusiasm for an egg's worth of candy.

But Esther and I were a sneaky pair. We soon devised a way to get rid of some of the beans. When she wasn't looking, we would pour a handful down a snake hole. "Well, children, air we already done?" Wonder what she thought when those beans sprouted and started growing out of that hole.

Her shoes were scuffed and one heel slanted one way while the other slanted in the opposite direction. There was usually a gash in the toe of the shoe, allowing room for an expanding corn. In reality, when she was dressed in her "Sunday go to meetin' clothes," she was a very pretty woman. I always thought if I could touch her face, her skin, even though she had wrinkles, would be so soft to the touch. But we were not a demonstrative family. Either side. Grandad would like to have been affectionate, but that was not Granny's nature. In fact, when we would go see Aunt Margaret or Aunt Minnie Lee Cooley or some of his other sisters, they always made over him (that's Pollard talk for kissing and hugging) and we knew that Granny was uncomfortable.

Personally, I think she felt it was sech foolishness. When Uncle Henry and Aunt Sarah drove to Pollard for a Sunday visit, Aunt Sarah always hugged and kissed Mother and Granny. Neither was very receptive to that. In fact, they were so scornful of such a display of emotions that it was years before I could hug a friend. Several years ago on a trip to Nicholasville, I went to see a second cousin with whom I had grown up. I envisioned a warm smile and a big hug. Shoulda known better. And that reminds me of the time Uncle Henry drove up in a bran spankin new 1935 black Plymouth sedan. We walked down to express our admiration and Grandad, who never smoked unless visitors were around said "Victor, run up to the house and git my cigareets." He put one in his mouth, took out a kitchen match and raked it against the door of the car with no more thought than he would have a fence post. Uncle Henry said, "Owen, you'll scratch my car!" Grandad was so offended that he sulked for months.

I wouldn't say that Grandad was a hypochondriac, but he ordered every patent medicine advertised in the Lexington Leader, Farmer's Almanac or on the radio. One in particular supposedly cured every ailment known to man. It was a foul smelling, mustard brown powder by the name of Black Draught. He called it Black Drat. He would stick his tongue out, place a liberal pinch of the evil mixture on the tip, take a drink of water and down it would go. I could never understand how he did that.

We used coal in the fireplace and wood in the big cast iron stove in the kitchen. It required years of experience and some talent for cooking in this type of oven, for they had no temperature gauge. There was no better cook in Pollard than Granny. It's hard to believe we didn't walk around in a diabetic coma; if a recipe called for one cup of sugar, she used two. That reminds me of something I did to pester her. She kept brown sugar hidden, or so she thought, in the dining room cupboard. But I found her hiding place and would sneak in and eat half a box. When she was annoyed with either one of us, she talked so fast that she forgot who was in trouble. I was, usually. Victor never did anything bad. She even got our names confused. Listen to her, "Gwictor, you've been into my brown sugar again"! Off she'd go to get a switch and I'd run home and stay until she forgot about brown sugar. After a few days, I'd return and she would have some little task for me such as cleaning the lamp chimneys. We used coal oil lamps and the chimneys had to be cleaned every three or four days. Wicks required trimming often, or lamps exuded black soot that clung to the inside of the chimneys. Since my hands were small, it was my lot to do the cleaning. Paper towels had yet to be invented, but newspapers and Sears Roebuck catalogs were a most efficient way to clean and this produced a sparkling, shiny effect. They were crumpled, stuffed into the chimney and turned around and around until the offending soot was gone. I am amused at some of the T.V. shows where coal oil lamps are used. The chimneys are always dirty and when the flame is extinguished they simply turn down the wick until it goes out. I haven't figured out yet how they do that.

There was always so much work to be done on a farm. Chickens had to be fed, eggs gathered, gardens planted and tended, and vegetables and fruit required canning or drying. I always managed to avoid all that peeling peaches, apples and pears. All I had to do was peel too much fruit along the peeling and that was a waste. But I did my share of carrying water from the cistern.

Cows had to be milked every morning and every night. Hogs had to be fed and slopped. On the back porch was the slop bucket, which was not to be confused with the slop jar. The slop bucket was kept in plain view on the screened in back porch and the slop jar was kept outside until just before dark when it was brought in and hidden under the bed. Both were an abomination. All leftovers (with the exception of Ol' Carl's dinner and supper) were poured into the slop bucket. Even used dish water-anything a hog would eat. And a hog would eat anything - except cucumbers. When full, the slop bucket was then carried to the hog lot and poured into the trough. The hogs squealed, fought and ate until it was empty. Then they wandered away until the next Here pig, Here pig. Speaking of that slop bucket, I was idly turning the pages of some high priced gardening catalogue when I saw a fancy metal bucket one could order for the purpose of collecting garbage and making compost. We had one for years, only it was called a slop bucket. And it definitely wasn't fancy. Nor did we need compost. Chicken manure and horse manure would make a stick sprout.

Daddy and Uncle Elmer often collaborated on some scheme to make money. Camp Nelson was a community about eight miles south of Nicholasville. Because of its unusual subterranean stream of water that surfaced at Camp Nelson - on the Jessamine County side, the distilling of spirits became a profitable industry. Mash was a by-product and was given to anyone with the means to remove it from the premises. Dad and Elmer loaded the truck with a huge galvanized tank, drove to Camp Nelson and filled it with the boiling hot mash. They hurried back to Pollard, and filled the hog troughs. Then everyone would climb up on the fence and wait for the fun to begin. The hogs would rush to the trough and immerse their snouts deep in the hot liquid. With a loud "BOOOSH!" they would back off until greed and hunger overcame their discomfort, then they'd try again. Still too hot. They'd squeal and back off again. I've said entertainment was scarce and that was great entertainment. Grandad had a saying. "Two things in life are certain. If you fool with barbed wire, you'll always get stuck and if you fool with hogs, you'll get shit on."

When Vic was attending the University of Kentucky, his Geology professor, Vince Nelson, was of a mind to have a party and serve a whole roast pig as an entree. Knowing that Vic was from the country and had access to pigs, he talked him into bringing him a nice roasting size shoat. That's a teen-age pig. Daddy still had that 1932 four door Dodge, so they tied the pig's legs together and placed him in the back seat for the ride from Pollard to Lexington. The combination of a first time motor excursion and having all four legs immobile, brought about an involuntary bowel movement that resulted in a forever-foul smelling car. However, Dr. Nelson's party was, as we sometimes say, "Another huge success."

Washday was every Monday morning. It was a big production-none of this throwing a few pieces of clothing in a washing machine and letting it do the work. Since running water was for city folk, we had to carry bucket after bucket from the cistern and of course, it had to be heated. Inside, on top of the stove in winter, outside in a big black iron kettle in summer. After the water was heated to the boiling point it was poured into a big galvanized washtub and the soiled clothing was set to soak. After it had cooled enough that our hands didn't become scalded, the scrubbing process began. A wash board was placed in the tub, the dirty garment was rubbed with homemade lye soap, then rubbed up and down, up and down over the corrugated ridges of the board until clean. It was then placed in another tub of clean "wrinch" water to which bluing had been added. This was a heavy blue liquid that supposedly made white clothes whiter and colored clothes brighter. The clothes were then hung outside on a wire clothesline. Clothespins were taken from the clothespin bag and snapped or slipped over all the clean clothes. They were then left to dry and nothing ever smelled better than sun dried clothes. An occasional rainstorm would send everyone hurrying outside to gather in the wash before it got wet.

Speaking of washboards, one year someone asked Bude Hager what he gave his wife for Christmas and he said, "a warshboard."

Everything, except underwear and socks, was ironed. Granny probably ironed Grandad's underwear. I happen to know that she made them for he just wasn't built for ready-to-wear. Most everything was heavily starched. With the exception of Grandad's underwear. Starch was made by boiling water, then stirring flour into the hot water and boiling until clear. Almost everything that we used was homemade. These starched clothes then had to be sprinkled with water, folded tightly and left to season for an hour or two before ironing. Of course, we had no electric irons. There were heavy flat irons that required heating on a hot stove. A thickly folded pad was wrapped around the handle for when the iron was set on the stove to heat, handle and all became very hot. Mother picked up the iron, turned it upside down, wet the tip of her finger and quickly touched the bottom of the iron. If, upon contact, a hissing noise was made, the correct temperature had been reached and the ironing began. That iron was used until the heat was gone; it was then placed upon the stove for reheating while a hot one took its place. Everyone had three or four irons. Mommy Johns was so frugal that she used every bit of heat in those irons. She would place an old dish rag on the ironing board, and tell Esther. "Here, child, rub over this a little bit." The iron was already lukewarm, but she used it until it was stone cold.

In March, it was time for spring house cleaning. That meant new wallpaper; lace curtains were taken down, washed and starched, and put on the curtain stretchers. No one ever tried to iron lace curtains. Feather beds were taken out and aired. A fresh coat of paint was applied to floors, windows and even some furniture. Kitchen chairs and tables had many layers of paint over the years. A little chip here and there reminded us of year before last's color.

Another little task for me was to gather in the eggs. I was somewhat apprehensive when doing this, especially if the hen was still on the nest. A settin' hen gets very possessive of her eggs and pecks hands and arms and if she really gets mad, her wings automatically spread out, feathers fluff and she looks like a big hen balloon. That's scary stuff to a little child. Chickens are the dumbest creatures. Granny had two lovely yellow rose bushes in the front yard and every time it rained one old hen and her brood would try to take shelter under one of the bushes. Of course they couldn't all be protected under her outspread wings and about half drowned during the downpour. After three or four years of this, Granny had the roses cut down. A good crop of chickens was more valuable than a rose bush.

As soon as Mother or Granny noticed that some old Dominecker hen was showing her maternal instinct by refusing to vacate her nest while clucking, pecking and fluffing her feathers, they knew she was ready to hatch her spring brood. Seventeen eggs were placed in her nest and the brooding period began. I could hardly wait for the first hatching of little chickens. They were so soft and cuddly and it was such fun playing with them. Of all the farm animals, kittens and little chickens were my favorites. Cows would never let anyone get near their calves, and little pigs were cute, but I was terrified of their mothers. If we did manage to pick up a little pig, it squealed as if we were killing it. Which is what we did - eventually. But little chickens did grow up to be messy and dirty and as they were not confined to one area they left their dirty mess all over the yard.

Chickens were a valuable source of meat. Our Sunday dinner in the summer time consisted of fried chicken and gravy and every vegetable grown in the garden. First of all, would be leaf lettuce, radishes and green onions. Next to make an appearance would be new potatoes and tiny green peas. From then on, until October, there were tomatoes, green beans, corn, beets, big fat butter beans and in the fall sweet potatoes, turnips, kale. All this had to be canned. Nothing was wasted. When Mommy Johns canned peaches, she peeled them, put them in jars and saved the peelings to make jelly. We had no freezers. Apples were peeled, sliced, and spread on a clean sheet. They were then taken out in the hot summer sun for drying. Mother and Granny made the most delicious fried apple pies. Granny made plain dried apple pie at least once a week in the wintertime. Everything we ate was seasonal. Packaged frozen food had yet to be invented. We had canned fruit and vegetables in the winter and fresh fruit and vegetables in the summer. Granny even canned strawberries; I didn't like them because they were mushy.

I never ate dumplings then and don't eat them now. Everyone thought Granny made wonderful dumplings except me. I've never thought dumplings were anything but wet dough and Lord knows, I can't eat anything that's not done in the middle. We often had Jell-O and real whipped cream for dessert. That was during the winter. Every kind of cobbler known to man was served in summer during the week.

Mother made the most delicious brown sugar dessert. Piecrust was cut into a square, a dab of butter dropped in the middle that was covered with brown sugar and flour. The crust was folded over, and baked in a hot oven until about half done, then she poured boiling water over that and finished baking until brown. The boiling water, brown sugar and real country butter combined made a most delicious "surrup." I never learned how to make that. She even drew a diagram showing how the pie dough was folded, but since she never measured the ingredients--a pinch of this-a handful of that, etc. Oh, and while I'm speaking of surrup, most everything sweet that could be eaten on a biscuit was called "sweetnin." If we wanted blackberry jam, we said, pass me the sweetnin'.

Our all time favorite summer time dessert was pineapple ice cream. This was served almost every Sunday. Daddy drove the eight miles into Nicholasville, went to the ice plant where he bought a fifty-pound block of ice. This was wrapped in newspaper and a gunner (gunny) sack. He also bought the Sunday paper and we enjoyed the Katzenjammer Kids, Maggie and Jiggs and other comic strips. While he was gone, Mother or Granny would have the ice cream mixture ready to freeze. As soon as he returned, the ice was chunked up with the ancient ice pick, the cream mixture poured into the freezer bucket, paddle was inserted, and it was capped and set into the wooden freezer. Next came a layer of ice, and a layer of salt, a layer of ice, and a layer of salt until the freezer bucket was covered. The remainder of the ice was placed in the old icebox, and a few bottles of beer were laid on top to cool. This was done while Mother went to church. Half an hour later it was cold enough to drink. Dad could swallow a bottle of beer faster than any fraternity boy I ever knew. In the meantime, it was my job to turn the freezer until the hard freeze stage then some adult had to complete the job. After about five more minutes, it was time to remove the paddle and pack with more ice and salt. It was then left to ripen until dinnertime. Grandad always picked out the pieces of pineapple before he ate the cream as he called it. Ay, he couldn't go that pineapple, but he sure did like the flavor.

We might have potatoes cooked three different ways. One person liked mashed potatoes while someone else preferred fried potatoes, and there were always potatoes cooked with green beans. These vegetables were cooked with a piece of middlin' meat and were simmered on the stove at least three hours. And I'm sure there wasn't a vitamin left in them! On cold winter days pinto beans were often left on the old iron stove all day. Biscuits were always served for breakfast and corn bread for dinner. Occasionally, both were served for dinner. Daddy liked cherry preserves and biscuits for breakfast. Of course, the cherry preserves were homemade and he refused to eat any that could be poured out of the jar. Like one popular brand of catsup, the spoon or knife had to stand straight up. We always had sorghum molasses for winter breakfasts. There is only one correct way to eat sorghum. First, you get a clean plate or saucer. You don't want your sorghum to taste like gravy, ham or eggs. Then cut off a big chunk of freshly churned butter and over that pour a liberal serving of sorghum. Mix it together with your knife blade, break open a good hot biscuit and use the same knife to smear a big dollop of molasses on the biscuit and forget about cholesterol. Speaking of biscuits, Mother never used a recipe. Women of that era were probably born knowing how that particular task was to be done. She used the same aluminum pan as long as I can remember. It had curved sides and a flat bottom. Into this she poured a few cups of flour, made a hole in the middle of the flour, added a pinch of salt, a pinch of baking powder, some lard, as much buttermilk as she felt was needed, then, with her right hand, worked the mixture into a ball of biscuit dough, leaving enough flour in the pan for the next time. She rolled the dough about a half-inch thick, cut out the biscuits, and then wadded all the little leftover scraps into various shapes and sizes. Daddy called them Pollies. In the early years of our marriage, I frequently made hot biscuits and our children enjoyed the little Pollies. They always asked why he called them Pollies and I never knew. They are an endangered species for I have never found a Polly in a can of biscuits. Bill said they are definitely an endangered species around our house. I might have to revive that custom for our grandchildren. Maybe. But then they'd ask why they were called Pollies. And I would have to say "Whee, why, just why that's why."

When growing up on a farm, food was never a problem. Money was scarce, we never had big homes or fine furniture but I can never remember being hungry.

A story about chickens would be incomplete without my telling about their most disgusting habit. All children in Pollard went barefooted in the summertime. In fact, I've never outgrown that liking for unshod feet. Chickens roamed the yard, the orchard, and the barn lot. The one thing those bare feet had to be on the alert for was a pile of fresh chicken droppings. Better known as hen doins. Now there are two kinds of hen doins. The first is a fairly mild smelling dump and while no one actually wanted to step in it, could easily be cleaned while rolling one's toes through the weeds or grass. The other, known as black hen doins, was a most odious mixture, which sent one gagging to the nearest creek or pond. This was to be avoided at all costs and it was only after several decades of city living that I learned to walk with my head up, not down, on the alert for black hen doins.

There's probably no creature on earth consumed by humans that is dirtier than chickens. Now I forgot about possums, but then we were never had to go that far down the food line. Chickens take dirt baths- of course, that's to suffocate any mites that are lurking in their feathers and then step and scratch in their own mess. Granny concocted some mixture to fumigate the hen house and kill mites but I can't remember what she used. Sulphur and something.

She had a separate chicken coop outside the hen house where she kept frying sized chickens penned up for about two weeks. She fed them nothing but corn, firmly convinced that this diet would rid them of all their impurities. When she was ready to serve fried chicken, she reached in the chicken coop, grabbed the cackling squawking fowl, which in turn started all the other prisoners into a cacophony of frenzied flapping, cackling, and squawking. She grasped it firmly by the head, and with a strong circular wrist movement, swung it around and around until the head came loose from the body, which then flopped around on the ground squirting blood for at least five minutes. When all movement had ceased, the unfortunate bird was immersed in boiling water to loosen the feathers. After being picked clean, it was then cut up into everyone's favorite piece. Mother couldn't have killed a chicken if we were starving. She wouldn't hurt a fly, and Granny could never understand why Mother couldn't kill a chicken.

After Daddy died and she moved to town, one of her neighbors asked her if she wanted a mess of fish. She did, but didn't know they were still alive. That really put her into a quandary, because she "couldn't kill the poor little things."

It was from Granny that I learned to soak chicken over night in salt water to get rid of the feathery taste. She never had a second thought about building a fire in the stove, frying chicken and making biscuits and gravy for breakfast. Sliced tomatoes were served also and if we wanted a taste of something sweet, there was always blackberry or raspberry jam, peach preserves, and if I had not eaten all of the Concord grapes, there were usually grape preserves. She and I had coffee, but for some reason Grandad had decided that coffee was bad for him so he had a cup of steaming hot water, poured from the big tea kettle which always sat on the back cap of the stove. He poured a spoon full of sugar in his cup, stirred it, and then saucered it until it cooled enough to sip. As he sipped from his saucer, he made a slight slurping sound, which I can still hear. All I have to do is close my eyes and imagine that I am back in their kitchen where Granny sits at one end of the long table, Grandad sits in the middle and I sit between them. It's not at all hard to do.

Our next plentiful meat was pork. Now known as the other white meat. I remember when Daddy would go hunting and bring home rabbit and squirrel, but I don't remember eating either. He knew exactly where to look for wild mushrooms. He'd bring home a big basketful, Mother would dip them in flour or meal and fry them in hot grease and he would have a feast fit for a king.

One of our favorite winter meals was dried beans and cornbread. Mommy Johns filled an iron kettle with dried beans, water and middlin meat on the stove every morning in the wintertime and Esther always had a bowlful when she came home from school.

Reynolds's Store

RURAL LANDMARK AND SITE OF CONSIDERABLE HISTORY is the Garland Reynolds' General Store at Pollard. The RFD 2 Nicholasville business finds the owner's granddaughter looking around from doorway.

Reynolds Store

Hugh Peel operated the first store on the site, about 1850. It was burned before 1891 and the business was taken over by my Great Grandfather, Milford Fain, and moved across the pike. A post office was then part of the operation. Legend has it that the postmaster came to the store to act on his official duty and give the post office a name. "How 'bout Fain?" Grandpa suggested. The postmaster told him that there already existed a Fain post office in eastern Kentucky. Great Great Grandpa Pollard Fain walked in and introduced himself and the postmaster declared it the Pollard post office. Therefore the community was called Pollard as well.

Pollard and Mary Ann Fain tintype photo

The store was sold in 1909 to Monroe Miller, and was operated by him until 1910 when it burned again. Monroe had owned a carriage shop across the pike on Peel's original site and after the fire, he moved his retail wares to the ground floor of his carriage shop and relocated the carriage shop upstairs. This business had been in operation for a long time under a Mr. Gayheart. He built new buggies and repaired old ones. He was also an excellent gunsmith.

Uncle Roland and Uncle Clay recollected that Gayheart had once teamed up with a man named Cook to make counterfeit coins. Cook and a third man occupied a large log cabin down on River Road. There they cast coins, which were then taken to the mountains to buy cattle.

The federal government became aware of the counterfeiting, but was unable to obtain evidence because the cabin had lookout windows on the upper floor and one person was always on the lookout while the coins were being made. If anyone came near the evidence was quickly hidden. Finally an F.B.I. agent was able to obtain his evidence by trickery. He became the fourth man to join the team. Soon he had collected enough evidence to convict both Cook and his assistant, but was unable to determine who made the molds.

One day he deliberately broke a mold while Cook was away. When Cook returned he reportedly remarked, "Don't worry, the man who made these is up at Pollard, he can repair them."

With this evidence, Uncle Clay and Uncle Roland concluded, Gayheart was arrested, convicted and sent to a penitentiary in 1870. Cook eluded authorities for a time, but was finally intercepted by 6 soldiers who had orders to bring him in dead or alive. They chased him across the river to Madison County where they shot and killed him.

Gayheart, after serving his sentence, once repaired a muzzleloader for Grandpa Johns. Grandpa, commenting on his fine workmanship, said, "With that talent, you ought to be able to make money." Gayheart sadly replied, "I tried that once and went to the state pen."

Monroe and his wife, Dorie, had two daughters, Ocie, and Nannie B. Dorie was very helpful in treating some of the local children for cuts, bruises, pulling teeth, etc. My second cousin, Jeanett Fain almost severed a finger making doll furniture. Dorie soaked the finger in coal oil and it soon healed. Jeanett has a scar but still has her finger.

Everyone thought Dorie was dirty because she liked cats and allowed them in her kitchen. My mother would never have allowed her to pull a tooth of mine. She thought cats were dirty and I agree with her. I only have to see a cat attending to its personal hygiene one time and then I wonder how a person can kiss an animal.

Garland Reynolds bought the store in 1934. Over the years, it has had several owners, but I will always remember it as being owned and operated by Garland and his wife, Virginia. Miss Gin, as I called her, worked in the store during the summer months and taught at Pollard school when school was in session. When no paying customers were in the store, she always sat on a stool, drinking co-cola and trying to work a crossword puzzle. My mother, who had a soft heart where children were concerned, could hardly bear to see her drinking a coke, when there were small children around. "You know they want some, and don't have any money to buy it."

The store had a front porch the width of the main part of the store. There was always a nail keg or two to be used as seats for the loafers. There was a gasoline pump at one end of the porch. The pump had a glass tank through which one could observe the level of the gas lowering as it was being pumped into one's vehicle. Gasoline sold for about twelve cents per gallon.

As I entered the store, a turn to the left brought into view a tempting array of cookies and candies, such as Baby Ruth bars, and marshmallow peanuts. There were different flavors of chewing gum and blow gum. Later known as bubble gum. My favorite cookie was a fat round marshmallow with a cake like crust. They were pink or white and covered with coconut. The white ones resembled a snowball that had been sliced in half. Well, I was partial to Bit O' Honey, also. These cookies and all the unwrapped candies were kept in clear glass containers inside a big glass covered candy case. If I wished to buy a cookie or a piece of candy, I gave Garland an egg that I had carried in my hot little hand all the way from Granny's hen house. Eggs were used as a monetary unit and were carefully hoarded by housewives to purchase items not grown on the farm. With one egg, I could buy two cents worth of candy or gum. After taking the egg, he simply reached inside the container, picked up the goodies and handed them to me. Since this was an era when health inspection had never been thought of and the government did not have its nose in everyone's business, merchants were not required to use metal tongs or clear plastic gloves. In those days, few people were germ conscious, anyway. That is, with the exception of my mother. She was always afraid that Garland's hands weren't as clean as they should have been.

Next to the candy case was the counter where customers stood to place an order. If Granny happened to spending an hour or so at the store, she always stood at the counter to see what everyone purchased. She was more than a little bit nosy.

On the other end were the scales with their iron weights where Garland weighed the thick slices of baloney and cheese.

The store also served as a restaurant. Customers came to the store and ordered a slice of baloney on lightbread, which was what we called bought bread. They would on occasion, order "fixed-up" pork and beans. "Fixed-up" meant to open a can of beans, pour in a jolt of vinegar, salt and pepper the mixture, and stir well. Don't knock it 'til you've tried it. They were eaten with crackers. This, washed down with a Co-Cola, Pepsi or Grapette and topped off by a Moon Pie for dessert made a very filling if not nutritional dinner. No matter, no one in that rural area had ever heard of the basic four. Big Ernest Miller came into the store one day and ordered the usual, with the exception of the Pepsi. When Garland asked him if he wanted a Pepsi, Big Ern said, "No siree, hit swells me!"

The first store bought pies came to the groceries about the mid thirties. They were packaged with a thin pasteboard bottom that looked just like the piecrust. Mr. Ed Mulcahy bought one to try and after eating it and the pasteboard, said, "It's good, but the crust shore is tough."

In the middle of the store was a big cast iron stove. Around the bottom of the stove was built a wooden frame, which was filled with ashes. It was about twelve inches tall and five feet square. Its sole purpose was to accommodate the tobacco-chewing loafers who were too comfortably ensconced on a nail "kag" or straight-backed chair to make the trip to the front door and spit outside. It was easier to spit in than a brass spittoon - more leeway.

On the right side of the store was the other counter. This one had a yardstick nailed tight for the purpose of measuring rickrack, lace and piece goods. Its surface was smooth and satiny and totally devoid of splinters because that's where the loafers sat when all the chairs and nail kegs were occupied. On that side of the store were shelves that held shoes, galoshes, gloves, scarves and handkerchiefs. Upstairs were tires, tools and other supplies. Underneath a back room was a space where chickens were confined until they were taken to town and sold. There were no animal rights activists in those days. When Victor was about fourteen, Garland hired him as a janitor and gofer, as in gofer to catch them chickens. He said that was the messiest place he had ever been in his entire life.

If someone had an accident or any unusual adventure, there were always interested and eager listeners sitting around the big cast iron stove. Victor was twelve or thirteen when the first movie with a synchronized sound track was shown in a Lexington theater. No one in Pollard had ever heard of such goin's on, except dad, who knew everything that was going on. He and Victor went to see the first talking picture. It never occurred to him to take Mother and me. Although, in the interest of fairness, she wouldn't have gone, because that would have been a waste of money. After seeing the talking picture, their first stop was the store where Victor told anyone who would listen how exciting it was to sit inside a building and see moving pictures of people as they emerged upon a screen facing the audience. He described the thrill of the talking pictures and as he excitedly talked on and on, Ol' Man Rufe Fain finally reached the limit of his endurance. He interrupted with, "Ay, God, that's a lie! Thar ain't no picture 'at can talk!"

The Pollard loafing society was a very humorous group of men. During World War II, many items were rationed, such as gasoline, sugar and meat. Each family was issued a ration book with a certain number of coupons and each coupon was worth so many points. For example, if Daddy needed gasoline, it not only cost money, it cost points. Few Pollard families bought meat, but if they did, ration stamps were required. In a roundabout way, I'm getting to another story. Holly Hurt's first wife, Mary, was a frail little lady, who had been in poor health for many years. She died prior to World War Two, and after a decent interval, Holly decided to marry again. This time, he chose a very healthy "womern" who, in Pollard, was called stout. He brought her to the store while several of the local wits were sitting around the stove. The bride and groom did their shopping and made their departure. Connie Hager looked around at his cronies, spat a stream of ambeer and said, "Well, it looks like Holly has got more meat there than he has got points." Holly, himself, was quite witty. One Pollard resident was so cross-eyed that Holly said his car didn't need a rear view mirror. Another Pollard widower decided he had shown proper respect to his deceased wife and had remained a bachelor long enough, but instead of finding someone his own age, married a sweet young thing. This resulted in several gossipy sessions at the store and finally someone mustered up enough courage to ask him why he didn't marry someone closer to his own age rather than robbing the cradle. "Wal," he said, "because I'd a heap ruther smell perfume than liniment."

Pat Burton was in his seventies when he started courting a woman in her thirties - even took her to Florida on a vacation. On his return, he told Clyde Teater about the joys he had experienced. "I felt like I was twenty one again", he bragged. Clyde laughed and said, "You just didn't feel in the right place."

Ode Hager hired on as the Nicholasville jailer (or was elected) for a term and when one female inmate told him she needed a box of Kotex, he told her to eat corn flakes like the rest of the inmates.

Roy B. Miller had learned how to cut hair when he was in the army and after the war was over, Roy B. often brought his barbering tools out to the store where he would cut hair for anyone who needed a haircut.

The store was an entertainment center as well as a place to buy groceries. Every Saturday night, couples would walk to the store to listen to the radio or to play checkers or to catch up on all the news of the neighborhood. Mothers brought their babies with them for there was always someone who wanted to love and admire a new baby. There was no such thing as Pampers. Soft well-worn sheets were cut up to make didies or hipp-ins. As in 'that baby's wet, hit needs a dry hipp-in'.

But of course, babies got hungry and then they were returned to their mama who discreetly opened the front of her dress and plugged him on. Some mothers weren't discreet and didn't even try to cover a milk swollen breast. When one breast was emptied, a quick inhalation and shrug of the shoulders brought it back in the dress and the other one was out before the baby hardly knew he'd been switched to the other side. And that was entertaining. Any male who had been raised right, turned his head or walked to another part of the store and then there were those who kept their eyes downward, but sneaked a look now and then. That was the custom back in those days and I tell myself that after having borne four babies, endured several surgeries and undressed for innumerable X-rays that I don't have a smidgeon of modesty left, but I don't think I could possibly have done that.

In the summertime, there was usually a game of horseshoes in progress. I was a pretty good horseshoe pitcher and if there were young people having a game, I was allowed to watch. But if there were only men enjoying a game, I didn't bother to ask if I could watch. Mother wasn't about to let me go down there where there was sure to be betting and cursing.

All through my growing up years, the only telephone within a two-mile radius was in the store. It hung on the wall to the right as one entered the front door. It was a two and a half foot tall box like contraption with the mouth piece protruding from the front of the box. The receiver, connected to the box by a three foot long cord, rested in its own hook on the left side of the box. On the right side was the crank, which was turned to call the operator, who was called, "Central." When she said, "Number, please." We then told her a two or three digit number and our party would be on the line. We used this phone sparingly and never abused the privilege for most of the time it was used only in emergencies. No one of my generation could have envisioned riding along in a car or van, and having the technology to make a call with a cellular phone.

Victor tells the story of Uncle Roland and his first experience with a pay phone. He read the directions, which said, "Lift the receiver, place a nickel in the slot and tell the operator what number you want." The word number was faded and illegible. When the operator kept saying, "Number, number please," Roland said, "Number, nothing, I want my peanuts." Actually, Roland told that on himself. And I feel sure that was just one of his whoppers.

Garland sold fabric for twenty cents a yard and a spool of thread cost five cents. The spools were made of wood, not Styrofoam. When the thread was all used, the spools were saved and strung on a string and given to babies for toys. Few could afford to buy rattles.

Salesmen who came to these country stores were called "Drummers." They usually had some gimmick to show the loafers. Mr. C.V. Cowgill was making his rounds one summer, but prior to showing Garland his line of goods, he asked some of the local boys, Vic was in the group, if they had ever seen a petrified thumb. Of course they hadn't. From his coat pocket he removed a small velvet lined box. A hole had been conveniently cut in the bottom of the box and his thumb had been painted a gruesome shade of blue. Due to many weeks of practice the thumb happened to be in the box just as the lid was removed. They gazed in wonder until Mr. Cowgill felt the time was right, and then he jiggled his thumb. Burl Taylor said, "Well, I be dog!" and another bunch of country boys was taken in by a slick drummer.

Another Country Store was located about three miles from Reynolds's Store. It was owned and operated by Great Uncle Larkin Fain and his wife, Aunt Minnie. This one was known as L.D. Fain's Store. Their daughter, Robin, submitted its history, which was published in the Jessamine County Historical and Genealogical Society. She has generously allowed me the privilege of using parts of her story.

According to Robin, one of the big events of early spring every year was Wallpaper Day. Uncle Larkin sent someone to Lexington to buy a load of wallpaper from the Rosenbergs. It was put in one of the storage buildings and the date of opening was announced. Before dawn of the big day, women gathered, waiting impatiently for the room to be opened. Robin says that one cousin brought his mother and hoped for an invitation to have breakfast with the family. Once inside the building, one could often see a woman hold up a roll of paper, saying, "If anybody finds this pattern, I don't need but one more roll to have enough for my bedroom."

Uncle Larkin ran year 'round accounts with many customers who paid when their tobacco was sold. He usually gave the customer a pocketknife when the account was paid. Today, the customer would get a computerized statement and be charged interest to boot.

This store was also a community center, a loafing place in both summer and winter. I can remember when Granny hitched Old Mae to the buggy and she and I went visiting. We visited Aunt Donie for an hour or so, then came back and visited Aunt Minnie and Uncle Larkin.

During World War Two, customers were often disappointed because of shortages. One lady, Mrs. Ann Fain, who lived on Hickman Creek, came in one day to buy some underwear and when told they were unavailable said, "Lord God! They ain't fightin' the war with drawers, are they?"

Across the road in front of the store was the horseshoe pitching area. Aunt Minnie could sling a mean horseshoe and was the undisputed champion pitcher. She was one of my favorite great aunts. As an adult, every time I returned to Pollard for a visit, Mother and I always went to see Aunt Minnie. She greeted me by saying, "Come on in here, you still don't look a day over sixteen." Even when I was fifty! Going to see her was good for my ego. She never sat down as long as there was work to be done and I think that was one of the reasons she was happy to see us. She could rest and chat for a while. I loved visiting the Aunts and Great Aunts because I never got tired of hearing their stories. Once when we were visiting we were talking about how education has evolved over the years and she mentioned that when Uncle Larkin was a boy his teacher was Great Great Uncle Lark who thought absolutely nothing of using a switch on a child's behind for misbehaving. And Uncle Larkin liked nothing better than getting someone else in trouble. There was a man named Ely Stinnett who had no occupation but mostly prowled the hills hunting and fishing. So when Uncle Lark asked a student who discovered America Uncle Larkin leaned over and whispered "Ely Stinnett." So of course, the child called out, "Ely Stinnett." Uncle Larkin got a right smart spanking for being so smart.

Aunt Minnie made beautiful quilts. One of her creations "the flower garden" is registered with the Kentucky Quilt Society. Granny's sister, Aunt Ida, quilted until she was 90 and never needed glasses. Granny was behind the door when that talent was passed around, but no one could hold a candle to her when it came to cooking. She was actually known to be the best cook in Pollard.

Uncle Larkin ran the store every weekday except Christmas until his death in 1968. Aunt Minnie kept it open for two more years, and then it closed forever. She would never tell anyone her age but my mother knew her date of birth. During a stay in one of the Lexington hospitals some young doctor walked into her room and asked, how old are you, Mrs. Fain? She told him it was none of his business. She lived to be ninety-five and she and Uncle Larkin are buried in the House graveyard on Pollard Road.

Mother's Diaries

My mother was very diligent about writing nightly in her diary. There was enough space for five to seven day's events on each page. In reality, there were very few events listed. One would think that these diaries would contain information helpful to me in writing this little story. Not so. They consist of very impersonal chronicles of the day's activities. There was always a short weather report, for example, A beautiful day. Or on another page, It poured the rain.

Calvin and Garland went to the mountains today. "I cleaned Mommy's house." Or Dallas and Mayme came and canned tomatoes for Mommy.

Four out of five entries had some reference to food. "I cooked pinto beans for Victor's family today."

Or, "Jean brought over two chickens for me to fry for her family." In her later years, Uncle Herbert and Aunt Mayme would have starved had she not cooked for them.

Most everyone shared garden produce with their neighbors. Mother always said, "They divided with me."

Occasionally, at the top of a page would be written the word "<u>DEATH</u>" Capitalized and <u>under lined</u>. Somewhere in those five to seven entries there would be a short account of some one's passing on to the other side. "Connie Hager died at Arthur's." (Arthur was Connie's brother.)

Once she recorded tersely, "Calvin left home drunk; came home drunker." There was no weather report that night. The next two pages were ripped out. That entry was sometime during her fifty-seventh year and she must have regretted writing it for in a later one where she recorded her birthday presents, I read "and a percolator from my dear husband."

Every other week would be a notation that Gwen had called. Every two years, the opposite would be written. I Called Gwen. That generation did not believe in wasting money (Sniff) on long distance telephone calls.

In the spring of nineteen eighty, she was quite ill for several weeks. Still she wrote dutifully every night. During this illness, friends and neighbors visited; many bringing food and flowers. She recorded each, usually with gratitude. However, one second cousin had over stayed his welcome, for the entry that night proclaimed, "So and So came to see me, stayed three and a half hours and worried me to death. Or about." And I see no reason to tell who that was. Oh, I might as well, it was Dr. Wylie.

She almost never wrote anything of a personal nature in her diary. One would think she would write how she felt about an unfaithful husband who had at least two other women. That she knew about!

I don't know how, but I was aware at a very early age that he was seeing other women. Once, when I was about six, as he was leaving, I said, "Daddy, take me to see your other woman.' We were at Granny and Grandads when that happened. Believe me that caused more uproar than a weasel in a hen house.

She always wrote about attending church. There were more references to food, though, than any other topic.

They also contained other interesting little tidbits. For example, on the very last page of one five year diary, was the written the recipe for homemade liniment. "You take one cake of camphor, one egg, three tablespoons coal oil, three tablespoons vinegar and one tablespoon turpentine. Put all together (shave camphor) and shake well." If I thought it would help my aching back, I'd be shaving camphor right now.

Another was "set hen today." And still another, Big Tit had calf today. Obviously Big Tit was one of the cows. Another cow must have resembled a goat, because she was referred to as "Goat Cow." Goat cow's calf died today.

I get these dairies out occasionally and try to read between each day's three or four lines. I wonder what else she was thinking as she recorded these little short entries, and I'll probably always wonder how she felt about me for we were never close enough to put words into feelings or feelings into words.

However, I am aware that if I ever feel the need to know what the weather was like in Jessamine County, on June 16, 1965, it is recorded in a little dark green book with gold embossed pages, which I keep in my top dresser drawer. And I'm sure that someone divided something with my Mother on that day also.

That Ol' Time Religion

The first 'churches' in Pollard were simply revivals in area barns. Grandad's brother, Uncle Elijah, familiarly known as Uncle Ligey, willingly consented to the use of his barn. However, Pollard residents felt the need of a real church building and set about to remedy the situation. Mr. Joe Reynolds sold the lot for $50 and Benjamin House 'stood' for $3,000. Uncle Dock Cobb was chairman of the building fund and asked the preacher if it would be all right to ask a drunkard for money. The preacher said, "Why not, it's been in the devil's hands long enough."

The founders of Mt. Beulah Methodist church were Benjamin House, (my great grandfather) Lindsay Stinnett and Henry Reynolds.

The church was dedicated in the spring of 1903, when guest minister George Ribald preached the first sermon. Services at that time were held once a month but since 1946 have been held on Sunday and prayer meeting every Wednesday evening.

All the members of that church deserve recognition, but only a few can be named here. Mrs. Mary Blakeman taught a Sunday school class for fifty years. She should have a gold star in her crown. Others deserving a gold star are my mother and Mary Miller for playing the piano for many years. Mother considered this an honor and a privilege instead of a chore. Roy B. Miller and his wife, Martha, have been stalwart members for over fifty years.

My earliest church related memory was the first spanking I had as a small child. I was sitting with my mother when I turned around and saw Grandad about four rows back. I wanted to go back and sit with him but was told "No." In those days a parent's "no" was to be obeyed at all costs and punishments for infractions were swift and to the point.

When I ignored her refusal and crawled under a number of church pews and climbed up in Grandad's lap, she didn't crawl under any seats, but she was waiting for me when I arrived at my destination. I was taken outside and the equivalent of a peach tree switch was applied to my legs. I can still feel the sting and to this day I know how to act in church! Grandad was so upset that he walked all the way out to our house the following day to check on me. As this story was told and told again down through the years, I always felt a warm feeling of love for Grandad because he was so crippled that it was no easy feat for him to walk such a distance. He was relieved to see that I had no red marks on my legs, and I knew that he really loved me because he was so concerned.

Spanking was one method of punishment. Parents couldn't use the threat of withholding television privileges for of course, there was no television. And they couldn't say, go to your room this minute, for most of us did not have a room. We simply had a place to sleep. One of the most effective means of punishment was pinching. If we were in church, or had company, it could be done inconspicuously and no one but the culprit was aware that he or she had been punished. Mommy Johns was a great pincher. All those years of milking cows and screwing on hundreds of jar lids every summer made Esther and me think she had a pair of pliers in one of those pockets. She'd grab a piece of arm or leg between thumb and forefinger; give a good hard twist and next day there would be a walnut sized bruise. This was not thought of as child abuse, it was known as making the children mind. Parents and Grandparents who did not discipline their children were derelict in their duty. Listen to them:

"You'd better mind me, now." Or simply, "Mind me." We even obeyed our aunts and uncles. Even worse than spanking or pinching was their method of shaming the guilty culprit. If we were caught committing a minor infraction, some adult might point a finger and say, "now, ain't you peart." It was said in such a scathing tone that we were immediately reduced to a red-faced mass of shame. Well, I got off the track there, but I do that about three times every day. Back to religion.

Attending Sunday school was mandatory. At that time, the church did not have separate rooms for classes, but classes congregated in different sections of the church where each teacher spoke quietly to her class. Our lessons were simple and easily understood; each with a moral that lasted a lifetime. At the end of the class, we were presented with the following Sunday's lesson. They were not printed in booklet form, but on a four by eight piece of cardboard. There was a Biblical scene on one side and the appropriate verse and lesson on the other. We soon learned every verse of "Jesus Loves Me" and other simple religious songs.

We carried a penny to put in the collection plate in Sunday school. Aunt Dallas was teaching the class one Sunday and asked "What happened to Lot's wife when she looked back?" Marie (Reedy) Hurt raised her hand and said, "she was turned into a cushion of salt'. Another time, Mrs. Mary Blakeman said, 'each of you tell me what you did for your mother this morning." One of my first cousins proudly announced that he had emptied the slop jar. And I might as well tell who that was. Wayne won't mind.

Easter was a day of celebration and I always had a new dress to wear on Easter Sunday. I remember one Easter when Mother had fashioned a pink pique dress for me that I absolutely hated. She had ordered a pattern from The Lexington Herald and I didn't like it from the first time I saw it. The sleeves were long and, at the shoulder, stuck up in a sharp point. I don't remember anything else about that dress except those sharp pointed sleeves, but that was enough! She had added a tad of starch and ironed them to make them even sharper. I walked as far as Mommy Johns' house mouthing to myself all the way, "I'd rather have a tick in my navel than to wear this ol dress." Suddenly I was overcome by a state of rebellion, and my right hand reached up to my left shoulder and that starched point was crumpled and wadded much in the same way as those slick glossy pages in the Sears Catalogue. The same treatment was given to the right shoulder. By the time I reached the church, those points were no longer sharp but Mother never did figure out what happened to her stylish design over which she had worked so hard.

Mother's Day was mostly celebrated by attending church. Very few mothers had children who lived far away, so there were no long distance phone calls and no one had telephones, anyway. Roses were always in bloom and if one's mother was still among the living, one wore a red rose to church. Wearing a white rose signified the opposite. I always felt so sorry for anyone who had to wear a white rose, and years later, after my mother died, I could not attend church on Mother's Day for about three years.

Methodism now is not as fundamental as it was then. Every summer, we had revivals that lasted for two weeks. These were usually held in the dog days of August and since electricity had yet to make its appearance in Pollard, there were no electric fans nor was there any air conditioning. Each pew did have several cardboard fans, which advertised various businesses in Nicholasville. However, the majority urged one to consider Betts and Smithers Undertaking Establishment should such services be needed. On the other side was a picture of the last supper or some equally well known biblical scene. On my most recent trip to Nicholasville and Pollard, Esther gave me one of those old fans dated 1949. The year Bill and I were married. It is a remnant from a funeral; I wish I knew whose funeral, but I am sure it was a Pollard funeral because it came from Mommy's house.

During revival time we children learned the books of both the old and new testaments and Bible verse drills were held prior to the service. For example, the preacher would open his Bible at random, call out the name of the book, chapter and number and the first child to locate and read the verse would be awarded so many points. We were also required to memorize Bible verses.

The seating arrangements during these revivals were almost pre-determined. First to enter the church were the most devout members. They always sat in the front of the church. They were also the most vocal. From those two rows came the shouts of, AMEN, BROTHER! Aunt Laurey Locker always sat on the front row and from her could be heard the plea, "Lord, help, Lord."

The lukewarm Christians occupied the next few rows. Neither real bad nor real good. Behind this group were seated the courting couples. Many lifelong commitments were formed during summer revivals. Notice that I did not use the word relationship because of what it implies. Well, back to that old time religion.

On the very back row sat the outright sinners. That was where Aunt Laurey Locker set her sights when the preacher issued the altar call.

Some of the younger men never entered the church. They enjoyed hanging around outside, telling tall tales and on occasion, standing near an open window and pestering a member of the congregation. One night, my cousin Herschel had a seat by the window and Uncle Roland was walking back and forth, making faces, pointing his finger, and acting a fool until Herschel could stand it no longer. He removed his shoe and threw it at him. That was a long time ago. Long before Gin chased Roland until he caught her. Also, long before he was saved and decided to memorize the entire Bible.

To set the stage for the beginning of a Hell Fire and Brimstone sermon, some of the old, old Methodists hymns were sung. Occasionally there would be an hour or so of public testimony. The preacher asked if anyone would like to stand and tell how being saved had changed his or her life. After a moments' hesitation someone made the first move. Aunt Laurey Locker was such a devout and fervent witness to God that the religious feelings of other members of her family were sometimes overlooked, but one night her husband, Walter, felt the need to give his own testimony. It was awe inspiring, for about halfway through, she could no longer sit still. She jumped up and said, "Tell it Walter, honey, tell it all, and don't leave a thing out!"

After the testimonials, it was time for the pre sermon prayer. Any Methodist preacher worth his salt could make that last for at least thirty minutes.

Next came the sermon, which was never shorter than an hour and a half. Few sermons were preached about the love of God. Most were filled with dire warnings of the fires of hell and it was a rare preacher who didn't know enough frightening stories about where we were going if we didn't repent and be saved. There was always one, sometimes two or three stories of some poor soul who had been thinking of getting saved, but had postponed it for some reason or another and wouldn't you know, he was struck by lightning or kicked in the head by a horse and now he has to spend eternity burning in hell. These stories were about people in some faraway place but emotion ran as high as if it had happened to our down the pike neighbor.

All of those old time Methodist preachers were yellers, and they didn't have a microphone hidden inside the pocket of their suit. They didn't need one. (And that's another thing, they wouldn't have thought of putting on a robe. That would have been too much like a Catholic priest.) Later, though, when I read the book "Old Yeller" I always thought about Brother Willie Peel. Only a very small child or an infant could sink in so deep a sleep as to be oblivious to his surroundings. It was said you had to be deaf, dumb and blind to fall asleep during one of Brother Willie Peel's sermons. You might think you were going to be able to nod off when he dramatically lowered his voice for a few minutes, but get ready, because any minute now he's going to pound on the lectern, shake his fist and shout, "ARE YOU LISTENING, SINNERS?" We are now!

After the sermon came time for the altar call. This was the purpose of the whole revival and time to start working on those back of the church sinners. Music played a big part. Hymn selection was very important. Few could resist "Just as I Am, Without One Plea." This hymn, by itself, was usually good for the conversion of two or three souls. But if no one repented then the preacher really got down to business. Soon he was coatless, and in his sweat soaked white shirt, he would step down from the pulpit and begin pleading, Oh, Sinner, won't you come, come before it's too late. Come, while we sing just one more stanza. Now by this time, Aunt Laurey Locker and her Lord, help Lord! was on her way to the back row because that preacher surely needed some assistance. She stood in front of some red-faced sinner and begged and pleaded until she realized that she was smack dab up against a brick wall. This particular one just wasn't ready to give up card playing, homebrew drinking and laying out. All the while - Just one more last stanza. At last, someone would walk up the aisle from somewhere in the church, kneel at the altar of God, and with the assistance of the front row Christians, would be prayed into conversion. Just one more last stanza.

After the "final" last stanza, family and friends gathered around the repentant, tears were shed, hugs were exchanged, more Lord, help Lords were said and sometimes it took and sometimes it didn't.

Being saved was a very emotional experience for the observer as well as the participant. As the observer, I was afraid Aunt Laurey Locker would start working on me, but she evidently didn't think my sins were black enough. (Even though I felt guilty until the next revival.) She always headed for someone in the back of the church, and of course I never sat in the back rows. This part of the service could last another hour, depending on how long it was before the light appeared. Then sleeping children were carried to a wagon or a horse and buggy, lanterns were lit in preparation for the long ride home over those dusty roads.

Not only were there revivals in Pollard; there were big time revivals in Wilmore. These were called Big Camp Meetings. Wilmore is a small town about five miles west of Nicholasville. Its main claim to fame was Asbury Theological Seminary, a small religious college where many Methodist ministers received their education. These students often supplemented their income and gained valuable experience by conducting Sunday services at small Methodist churches such as Mount Beulah and Mount Lebanon. Occasionally, the members would be fortunate in acquiring one with a modicum of talent but more often than not they were forced to sit through Sunday after Sunday with a young man who hardly knew the verses of the Bible. There were also some would-be preachers during World War Two who felt God's calling in lieu of Uncle Sam's.

Big Camp Meeting was held under an open-air tabernacle. This was a round roof supported by strategically placed poles. The ground underneath was covered by several inches of sawdust and long rows of bench seats. Seats were set up from back to front.

Word reached all of the surrounding communities that a revival was in progress. Pollard folks' transportation to Wilmore was by means of dad's or Uncle Elmer's flat bed truck. Always one to take advantage of the opportunity to earn a bit of beer money, Dad charged everyone a dime for the ride. The central meeting place was the store and Dad already had the cattle racks attached to the sides of the truck. Taking a 13-mile ride standing in the back of a truck on a scorching summer night was something to look forward to. The road was curved and narrow and sweethearts were always falling against each other.

People came to these meetings from far and wide. There was special music, bright, bright lights and every species of moth known to man was drawn to those lights. One Pollard character remarked that some were so large it took only six to make a dozen.

I never knew where Dad escaped to during these meetings; I do know he never attended the services. Wherever he went he was always back when we were ready to leave. If he took a notion to get a beer, he had to drive back to Nicholasville because you sure couldn't find one in Wilmore. Dad never attended church services unless it was for a funeral.

We children were given free rein to roam around the grounds for no child wanted to listen to a scary sermon about devils and the fires of hell. These preachers always preached that Heaven was a place where the streets were paved with gold and Hell was in the bowels of the earth. Satan resided there with his assistants, all armed with pitchforks.

My greatest fears were bears, panthers, and going to Hell. I wonder how much psychological damage was done to gullible young minds by some of those religious zealots. It sure did mess me up, for I have never known what to believe. Methodists believe one way,

Presbyterians another, and Lutherans still another and I've tried them all and still don't know what's going on.

If we could close our ears and not listen to the sermon, and most of us could, revivals were fun and highlighted the summer season. And if we were really bored, we could always watch Bob Angle pick his nose and I must have watched constantly, for in the Kodak area of my brain, I can see him as plainly as if I had a picture. Esther and I would really get the giggles especially if he happened to pull out one so large that it could have been used for an earring. One night, Esther asked, "Mommy, where's he gettin' all that from?" And Mommy said, "Hush, child and listen to the preacher." But I don't think she knew either.

Methodism was the only acceptable religion in that rural area. Catholics were heathens because they worshipped idols. And any good Methodist knew that worshipping graven images was strictly forbidden. Mother referred to them as, them ol' Catholics. Many years later, when she moved to town, she became much more tolerant and had many Catholic friends. She also discovered that not only were they very nice people, they had such wonderful Friday night fish fries.

Baptists believe in the doctrine that once saved, always saved and Methodists know that is a most ridiculous theory. Methodists are always backsliding and must be saved again and again. Backsliding means to revert to sinful ways. Some Methodists were known to be saved every summer during revival time, back slide during the winter, and repeat the process again the following summer. There were also the last resort conversions. If one had an illness that did not respond to the ministrations of Dr. Williams, then one turned to a Higher Power as a last resort. More often than not the body healed itself and as time passed so did promises that had been made. This gave rise to the saying, so and so is a whole lot better and is feeling well enough to back slide.

They were honest, hard working people who relied upon their church for their spiritual well being. All in all, Pollard folks were the salt of the earth.

Readin' Writin' and 'Rithmatic

The Pollard School

Pollard school was a two room building located in the exact center of the community. Grades one, two, and three were taught in one room and four through eight in the other. My Aunt Dallas Johns taught the first three grades. Every child should be so lucky as to have "Miss" Dallas for a teacher. She never lost her patience, and if a voice could contain a smile, hers did. Mrs. Garland Reynolds had grades four through eight. We called her Miss Gin. The title Ms had yet to be created, and if we were required to use the title -Mrs.- we pronounced it Mizriz. Miss Gin was a good teacher and I liked her, but I loved Aunt Dallas. So did everyone else.

Like schools of today, the teacher's desk was in the front of the room. Directly behind her was the blackboard. There the similarity ends. Our school supplies and equipment did not extend quite so far back as slate and chalk. But they were very primitive. Computers, TV screens, and word processors had never been envisioned. Our most complicated piece of equipment was the communal pencil sharpener. Hand operated, of course. This was nailed to the teacher's desk and we could break the monotony of learning the chief agricultural products of Brazil by taking a trip to the pencil sharpener and back to our desk. Provided that we didn't take advantage and do it too often. This was also a sneaky way to pass a note to the heartthrob of the moment.

Our classes were strictly Reading, Writing, Arithmetic, History, English and Geography. There were no extracurricular activities, such as Art or Physical Education. Walking to and from school and doing farm chores provided exercise. Any leftover energy was expended by running, chasing each other, jumping rope, or playing hopscotch.

We had no after school activities, such as soccer leagues, Little League Baseball, piano lessons, or drama classes. We went to school and that was it. We didn't have pre-kindergarten, kindergarten, pre-school, day care, - well, actually, we did have day care but it was mothers and grandmothers and Grandads.

I remember the layered look long before that particular style hit the fashion scene. Those one and two room schoolhouses had a central heating system - a pot bellied stove located in the center of the room. Girls always wore dresses to school and in winter a sweater, long underwear (also known as a union suit) and long stockings were required for warmth.

Long underwear was such a troublesome garment. As the name implies, the legs were long and ended just above the ankle. They had an opening down the front and a flap in the back that could be buttoned and unbuttoned. Every time nature called, that flap had to be unbuttoned and lowered. A small child had to be extremely careful to keep bloomers, underwear flap and long stockings dry. The underwear was to be folded neatly at the ankles and there was definitely an art to pulling the stocking up quickly to avoid bulkiness at the bottom. After being worn for two or three days, the underwear legs became stretched from putting on and taking off and even more skill was required. We could surmise how dirty our classmate's underwear was by the size of the folds in her stockings.

Those long stockings were the forerunner of today's brightly colored and lovely patterned tights. By no stretch of the imagination could they be called attractive. Their texture was ribbed and their color was an ugly shade of tan. A homemade elastic garter held them up. Occasionally, Miss Liza Scott Crutcher would be our substitute teacher. She was a rather thin lady who could never keep her hose up and the seams in back were as crooked as a dog's hind leg. They were always wrinkled and sagging around her thin little legs. We had no panty hose in those days. One day when I came home from school, Mother said, what on earth is wrong with your stockings? I told her that was the way Liza Scott wore hers. That had to be a first grade story because Mother told it all over Pollard and everyone thought it was cute.

Back tracking to the stove in the center of the room, older students could earn a bit of money by arriving at school early and building a fire. They were also called upon to shovel lime under the toilet seats. I think that was one of Victor's jobs. He was probably paid a nickel or dime a day.

Mt. Beulah Methodist church was practically next door to the school and two of my female second cousins had janitorial duties one year and Burl Taylor started "accidentally" passing by just as they were cleaning. Of course, he just couldn't resist stopping to talk and aggravate, so Jeanette and Ted (Ted was a nickname for Waveline) warned him that they would get him down and take his pants off if he didn't stop. He didn't and they did. Recently, Vic asked Burl if he remembered that and he said he'd never forget it. Vic asked how big he was at that time and Burl's answer was, not big enough or they wouldn't have done it. Even more recently I saw Burl while on a visit to Nicholasville and he informed me that there were three girls: the other was Rena Locker.

We were not transported back and forth to school on a big yellow bus. Neither did our mothers participate in a carpool. During my first few years of school, there were very few cars in the entire community, but they were used for a trip to town on Saturday or to go visiting on Sunday. From the time that Daddy took over Uncle Larks' car, he always owned a truck or car, but it didn't carry children to school. We walked. Snow, rain, whatever, we walked. A few of us might have owned a raincoat or an umbrella but the elements were inconsequential. I was fortunate that I had a short distance to walk.

Bathrooms were non-existent and so were water fountains. Our day's water supply was stored in a large aluminum container and each child was required to bring his or her drinking cup. My mother was paranoid about germs even in that un-scientific and un-hygienic era. "Never chew someone else's gum or never take a lick of some one's sucker. Never take a bite of some one's biscuit and jam." These admonishments were preached to me so often that I would have died of thirst before drinking from any cup but my own. This was permissible at home for we had a water bucket with its own dipper which was used by everyone in the family.

At the lower left corner of the schoolyard was the girl's toilet and the boy's was on the opposite side. I have no idea how the boy's toilet was constructed but the one used by the girls had a seat that was about two yards long. There were three holes carved that could fit only one part of the anatomy. Two girls usually traipsed to the toilet together. They would often hold hands and on occasion would walk with arms entwined, or with arms around each other's waist. Now in those days that only meant very good friends who enjoyed each other's company. It also meant they were there for mutual support, for as soon as Hansel House saw two girls on their way to the toilet he would wait until they were inside, then run behind the building and beat on the back side. This caused much shrieking and, hurriedly pulling up bloomers, the girls would run to tattle to Miss Gin.

Hansel kept all the girls in a tizzy. He was my first boy friend. Or at least I thought he was. I don't know what today's fifth or sixth graders do to be going together, but in those days, if a boy winked at a girl, that meant, I like you, will you be my girl? I was reading this to my irrepressible niece, Missy, and she interrupted with, they sleep together. But back to yesteryear. If the girl turned red and winked in return, that meant, Yes. This was what our parents called puppy love. It could last from one week to four weeks depending on how long it took Miss Gin to see the surreptitious note passing. During those courtship's, many trips were made to the pencil sharpener. What today's generation calls a relationship was then called settin' out. It was also called sparkin'. Settin' out probably stemmed from an old hen settin' out on her seventeen eggs.

It was very common for men and boys to have nicknames. They were usually in conjunction with some physical feature or personality trait. O'Neal True was one of my classmates. His nickname was "Shiny." He had shiny blond hair. Augustine Miller was another and his nickname was "Pooge." That was a derivation of pudgy, for he was certainly that. Garland's nickname was Doc. And I recently found out that Victor had a nickname. It was "Grandad." People were forever asking small children, "How old are you now?" And when Vic was five and someone asked him how old he was, he said, Grandad said I'd be 6 the 25th. So that was how he acquired the nickname of "Grandad."

Roberta Blakeman was the smartest girl in our class. Her assignments were always prepared on time. She also had a little brother who was called Sonny Boy. Betty Fain told me later that she didn't think Roberta was all that smart. The neatest and cleanest girl was my second cousin, Betty. Her parents were Great Uncle Iry and Aunt Annie (His real name was Ira Julian and his brother, Uncle Larkin, always called him Jude.) Betty always had the smoothest long underwear legs. I could hardly see the folds. She had long blond hair that Aunt Annie separated into just enough hair to wind around and around her finger; thus forming a long curl, which we for some reason called banana curls. I had straight brown hair, freckles and bulky underwear legs. I don't know why Hansel House ever winked at me, but he did, and that lasted off and on all through the seventh and eighth grades. Some of the other girls often tried to beat my time with Hansel, and usually they did. That translates into taking him away from me. It didn't require much effort, for he was a fickle sort and I had him one or two weeks, then someone else winked at him and he was all theirs until another one came along. He and Pansy Locker passed a few winks and notes, also. Her sister, Ruth, and Bobby Dean Wiley were sweethearts all through grade school.

Miss Gin and students, about 1938

Speaking of Betty's long curls reminds me of just how badly I wanted curly hair. Uncle Clay owned a sawmill and when we visited him and Aunt Laura, I'd pick around until I found some curled wood shavings, take them home and try to pin them into my own hair with bobby pins. They were fun to play with and imagine that I had beautiful curly hair, but they weren't very effective and also as soon as Vic saw them, he'd laugh at me and pull them off. About the only compliments I received pertained to my hands. I supposedly had nice hands and nails, and because of that, Vic would catch me and pop my knuckles and tell me that I would have ugly knuckles. I didn't care; when you've been "aggervated" by the best, namely Stringer, a few cracked knuckles didn't amount to a hill of beans.

Lunch was called dinner and since there was no cafeteria, we either walked home for the noon meal or brought it with us. I preferred to bring mine and eat at school so I could have time to play. Since at that time, education was not the frenzied effort to fill a child's head with encyclopedic knowledge, we always had a fifteen-minute morning recess and an hour at noon.

Favorite pastimes were jumping rope, hide and go seek, ante over, red rover and a form of baseball. The first two need no explanation. Ante over was a game of throwing and catching skill. Two teams were chosen and one team was on one side of the building; one on the other. A member of one team threw a ball over the building. When caught by someone on the opposing team, everyone on that side ran to the opposite side and tried to catch someone. When one was caught, he became a member of that team. The winning team was the one having the most members when it was time for Miss Gin to come to the front door and ring the school bell.

The baseball games we played were basically the same as today's softball games, with the exception of the ball and bat. The ball was always made of rubber and the bat was a flat piece of wood brought from someone's barn or from under someone's house. One end was whittled down to vaguely resemble a handle. This facilitated a tighter grip. We always played ball in the front yard of the school grounds for there were no windows in the front of the school building. It was great fun to hit a ball over the schoolhouse. That was an automatic home run. It was always a source of mild irritation that Ruth Locker was a better ball player than I was.

Dinners were carried to school in brown paper bags or in Karo Syrup buckets. Victor can remember his first day of school. I can't remember mine. He had a shiny new lunch box. (I don't know why he had a lunch box; I always used a paper bag. Well here's a perfect place to say that they always loved him best. I'll probably throw that in a few times here and there.) Granny had fried a chicken breast, boiled a ros'near, (that's Pollard parlance for corn on the cob,) and spread a biscuit with blackberry jam. At noon, he carried it outside and climbed upon the schoolyard fence, unpacked his lunch, and placed the chicken breast on the top of a fence post. "Granny B" lived directly across the road and like everyone else in Pollard, allowed her chickens free reign of the immediate area. One of her roosters smelled the food and hoping to get a crumb, strutted across the road. When Vic didn't divide, the rooster flew up on the fence, grabbed the chicken breast and flew back across the road. Poor Vic was left with a jam biscuit and a ros'near.

Winter apples were kept in cellars and usually lasted two or three months. So, a Karo syrup bucket filled with jam biscuit or sausage, an apple and a home canned pickle made a very fulfilling meal.

We took any leftover meat to school and were never concerned about refrigeration. Salmonella had yet to be discovered. What is now spoken of as a stomach virus was then referred to as a runnin' off. It was aptly named, for when one was afflicted with this malady one was often runnin' off to the toilet, or in some cases, off to the woods.

Country schoolrooms had an odor all their own. Combined with greasy meat and biscuits was the odor of unwashed children. Occasionally, there would be an outbreak of scabies, (then known as the eetch) and permeating both rooms would be the odor of sulfur and molasses. This, mixed together and applied to affected areas, was the accepted cure for the itch. I wouldn't know. I never had the itch nor did I ever have lice. Both conditions were thought to be the result of uncleanness. Granny and Mother certainly saw to it that I left home clean.

Permission to attend to nature's calling was obtained by holding an arm high in the air and waving in the direction of the teacher. If only the index finger was extended, that implied permission was needed to go to the toilet to do number one. Holding up the index finger and middle finger was the need to do number two. Number two was much more urgent and while a teacher sometimes ignored number one, those number two's got a quick nod and were out of there.

Those two or three holer outhouses always contained last year's Sears Roebuck catalog to be used for cleansing. Toilet tissue cost money. (Sniff) These catalogs had slick glossy pages and softer more pliable black and white pages. Needless to say, the black and white pages were used first. When necessity demanded the use of the slick glossy pages they were wadded and re-wadded until softened. If catalogs and newspapers were unavailable there was always a box of corncobs to be used for the same purpose. Vic says there was a box of red corncobs and a box of white corncobs. First used was the red one, then the white one to see if another red one was needed. That's another one of his stories that I'm not sure I believe. In fact, I'm not even sure I should be telling that one.

At the beginning of December, we started decorating the school for Christmas. Red, green, and white adorned every window. We cut out Santa Claus figures, white snowflakes and Christmas trees. Honey Comb bells were hung from the ceiling. Every year a huge cedar tree was cut from someone's farm and stood in Aunt Dallas's room. Having no electricity, we had no strings of brightly colored lights. But we did have paper chains, popcorn ropes and carefully hoarded colored balls.

Every year, we had a Christmas program to which parents were invited. This was called "having the Program." I can't remember my mother ever attending these Programs as she was usually in Lexington working at the Re-dryer. I stayed with Granny and Grandad and she was always there. For weeks we had been practicing our pieces, as we called the little poems and stories. The poems were memorized and the stories were read. Both were presented in a singsong monotone.

The festivities usually lasted about an hour, although to the impatient children, it seemed more like a week. At last it was over and Santy Claus, as he was called by country children, slipped in from somewhere and distributed gifts and listened to requests. Girls always asked for dolls, dishes or coloring books. Boys requested cap pistols, firecrackers or trucks. After talking to these shy, bashful children, he gave everyone a net stocking containing hard candy and a cheap tin whistle or something of equal value. For some children, in that post depression era, that candy filled stocking would be their only Christmas Gift.

Hog Killin', Cannin' and Preservin'

Every fall, as soon as the weather turned cold enough and there was no danger of a warm spell, people started thinking about hog killing. It was also a neighborhood get together for much assistance was needed. It was an all day job for the men and a week's work for the women.

The hog was brought in kicking and squealing from the hog lot, where his friends awaited the same fate, and shot directly between the eyes. Someone then slit his throat and the carcass was drained of blood. It was lifted into the hog box, which had been filled with boiling water, rolled over and over until the bristles were softened. They were removed by rubbing one's hands over and over the skin until it was clean and white and no trace of bristle remained. (It was said that Buanna Willis wasted nothing about the hog but its squeal, but for the life of me, I can't imagine what she could have done with the bristles.) It was then quartered into hams, shoulders, backbone, and middlin' meat. The intestines were placed in a big washtub, and the fat (called leaf fat) was stripped and put in a big black cast iron kettle and boiled until it was melted, it was then put in lard cans, where it congealed and that was our winter supply of lard. During one hog killing, I was standing around watching all the proceedings and Daddy looked at me and said, "Gwen, get over here and help your mother strip these guts." That was the only time in my life that I ever ran from my daddy. I knew he couldn't catch me and if and when I did get a whipping, it couldn't possibly be as bad as putting my hands in a tubful of hog guts. I later found out that he was only kidding. Middlin' meat was used to season pinto beans and any other vegetable. Pinto beans were called soup beans and were cooked two or three times a week during the winter. We had fried liver but I never ate that. Granny also cooked the brains with eggs and I couldn't even look at that! She used the head to make a sausage called souse. She placed it, minus the eyes, of course, in a fifty-gallon lard can, covered it with water and simmered it until done. She then stripped the meat and fat from the skull, ground it in a food chopper, added various spices and packed it into a loaf pan until congealed. It was then sliced, served with a jolt of vinegar and eaten with crackers. I most certainly never ate that but Victor pronounced it delicious.

My personal taste ran to fresh sausage and fried tenderloin. The sausage was made by cutting into squares what was trimmed from the shoulders and hams. It was ground in the sausage grinder, sage, red and black pepper, and salt were added, and it was then stuffed into sausage casings. They had been made from flour sacks and looked like small pillowslips. I always thought it so funny that Aunt Mayme didn't really like sausage until it had aged a bit; that was when I stopped eating it. I have Mother's recipe for sugar curing a ham. Who knows? Someone might buy a farm some day. It's probably cured in a microwave or some such contraption now. Here is her recipe in her own words:

> To cure a ham, take one pint of salt one tablespoon of black pepper one tablespoon of red pepper three tablespoons of brown sugar mix well. Rub the skin part with the mixture and fill the hock full and all over the other side. Have a big cloth spread, then news paper enough to wrap all around. Pin with straight pins. Place in a bag made from flour sacks and hang in a smoke house until cured.

I've never known why it was called a smoke house. We never smoked meat; it was always sugar cured or salt cured. It was better than smoked meat. Of course, that was a matter of taste.

Under the smokehouse was a deep dark cellar where the winter's supply of canned vegetables and fruit was kept. Mother and Granny also canned pork tenderloin and sausage. There were shelves, which held the winter's supply of canned beans, tomatoes, peaches, blackberries and all the other goodies that they had worked so hard to preserve last summer. They could make the best blackberry jam in the whole wide world. That was something I never accomplished. I always blamed my failures on the blackberries. The seeds were much smaller than the thornless varieties we have today and also we worked so hard to pick them and any job that required that much effort had to turn out a better tasting cobbler or cooking of jam.

Bushel baskets of apples, turnips, potatoes and sweet potatoes were also stored in the cellar. The only light was reflected from the coal oil lantern carried in one hand. This created horrible shadows and since I was always afraid of my own shadow, these other shadows brought a frog-sized lump to my throat. When I was sent to the cellar to get apples or a jar of pickles, it was with a pounding heart, for that was the darkest, dampest, coldest place on earth. I just knew the steps would break or the trap door would close all by itself and I would be down there forever. I imagined snakes and spiders and it wouldn't have surprised me to see a bear or two. (The Sky is Falling! The Sky is falling!) Nothing ever felt as good as emerging and seeing daylight again.

On cold winter nights Granny liked to get the old long handled wire popcorn popper from behind the kitchen stove and pop homegrown popcorn over the hot coal fire in the fireplace. When I was very small, I can remember her going to the cellar to get a pan of apples for us to have as a bedtime snack. As I leaned on her lap, she peeled an apple with a sharp knife, and then scraped it with a table knife and I ate it straight from the blade of the knife. It had the texture of applesauce. Grandad sat in front of the fire in his big rocking chair while we all listened to the radio. He always liked to listen to the news. Everyone who had a radio always listened to Lowell Thomas, then Amos and Andy and of course on Saturday night there was Renfro Valley, with Little Jimmy Dickens. We had to select our programs with care, and never carelessly leave the radio on because since we had no electricity, the batteries would run down. Waste not-want not.

Grandpa and Mommy Johns

Wedding Picture of William Johns and Cordelia House - 1892

Since Grandpa Johns died when I was two years old, I have no memories of him at all. I have only seen one picture of him and he was a very handsome man with eyes as black as prunes. He had the reputation of being a very good man and a learned man. (But I'll have to admit that I have my doubts about that, for he sure didn't teach those boys very much.) Their ornate Victorian bookcase was filled with books that he read but none of his children read. He bought one of the first radios in Pollard, battery operated and with only one set of headphones. Vic remembers sitting next to Roland, their heads together and he listened from one earphone as Roland listened from the other. Someone asked Grandpa why he only bought one set and he was informed that a body only needed one ear to hear with. Vic also remembered taking a sharp kitchen knife and going to the watermelon patch to thump for a ripe watermelon. Having found one he thought ready to eat, he nicked out a small bite. It wasn't and he told Grandpa it must have been a bird. Aunt Vina's twins remembered being deathly afraid of him. They had come for a visit when they were about four and as they played in the yard, he came out and sat on the back porch. They saw him and tried to avoid him by going in another door but he called "You twins come here!" They had no choice but to obey and all he said was, "Which one of you is Ruth and which one is Esther?"

Mommy Johns with Ruth and Esther

Uncle Clay's daughter, Mabel, was about 15 when he died and she also said she was afraid of him. But Victor remembers his being a kind and caring person. When he was about 5 years old, he stepped on a nail. At this time Mother and Daddy were living down at the Owl Den. Grandpa happened to be there and he carried Victor on his back all the way out to their house because he probably thought Mommy Johns knew more about "doctoring" than Mother did. I'm sure she used the old standby method by pouring a liberal amount of coal oil on the wound. That was the standard treatment for cuts and scratches back in those days.

Grandpa's father was a Baptist preacher and it seems fitting to include an article about him that appeared in a Kentucky paper many, many years ago. It was obviously written by a fellow preacher.

A Musical Shout

"During a meeting I conducted at Nicholasville several years ago, a strange brother came to the service that was a brimful of religious emotion. He punctuated the sermon with "amen's," and shouted while others prayed. I concluded that he was a religious fanatic and that if he ever got to heaven, the Lord would never hear the last of it. I asked Brother Stephen Noland who the man was. "He is old Brother Johns, and lives down among the river hills", Noland replied.

What kind of a man is Johns?" I enquired. "Well, said Noland, "The land down in those hills is very poor, and the people are poor, and Brother Johns is the only man there that I know that can make a respectable living. When the winters are severe, there would be a great deal of suffering among the people; but Brother Johns at such a time always offers his smokehouse and corncrib, and the poor are never allowed to suffer; that is the kind of a man that Johns is."

"Brother Noland", I said, "the next time that man comes to my services I want to meet him and tell him he can shout until the very rafters ring with his hallelujahs. That is the kind of shouting the world loves to hear, and no one ever tires of its music."

We loved Mommy Johns, but she had about two dozen other grand children, and Victor and I weren't at the top of her totem pole like we were at the other Grandparents. But she did go to the cellar and bring up a fresh jar of dill pickles every time I came to visit. She could make the best teacakes in the whole wide world. Some had white icing spread haphazardly and others were sprinkled with sugar.

Mommy's maiden name was House and most everyone born into the House clan was notoriously frugal. It was said that some of them were so stingy that they wouldn't give a dime to see a pissant eat a bale of hay. But that simply is not true. There is a difference in stinginess and frugality. And Mommy and Mother tithed at their church and were always willing to help a child or grandchild who had fallen on hard times. But Victor swears that some of the Houses (and Mommy was one of them) had a strange twitch at the mere mention of money. They inhaled a short, quick breath of air through the nose while simultaneously moving the upper lip sideways once or twice. This created an audible "Sniff" and a visible twitch. Vic doesn't know why they did this; I think it was an allergic reaction to the thought of having to part with their money. That particular gene was passed down the line to my mother, but skipped me entirely for I certainly do enjoy spending money. It lives on in Carol Ann, because she freely admits that she has a bit of "House" in her. (Sniff) Speaking of money, this generation might be interested in the fact that before Grandpa Johns died, he wrote his own will, which reads as follows:

Will of Wm. Johns

Nicholasville, Ky. March 8, 1928

I will that my wife Cordie Johns have the home at the pike including 13 acres more or less. I will that she have one thousand dollars ($1,000.) I will that she have the automobile. I will that she be the administrator of my estate and give the remainder of the farm to our seven children according to the allotment on the attached sheet, also what money may be on hand or may accrue to be divided between my seven children.

Wm. Johns.

I had the original copy of the will, (which Aunt Mayme had had framed) but the attached sheet dividing the farm has gone by the wayside. Everyone agreed that he was fair in his division of the farm, for there was no squabbling among the children. He died September 7, 1928.

In corresponding with my first cousin, Mabel Sturgill, I learned that Great Grandma House died at Mommy Johns' house. She fell from a chair while visiting Uncle Sam and Aunt Margaret and broke her hip. She stayed with them for a few weeks, until they felt another child should share the burden. So they moved her in with Aunt Francis and her husband, Mr. Harris. I haven't the faintest idea what his name was, for we never heard her call him by any name except Mr. Harris. After five months with them it was another child's turn. She was moved to Mommy Johns' to spend her remaining months. Not only did she have a six-year-old Esther to care for, that was the summer that Uncle Harry and one of his preacher friends (his name was Brother Pearson and before he felt the "Call", he was a railroad man) came to Pollard to conduct a revival. Of course, they stayed with Mommy and she had no help, so she prevailed upon Mabel to help with the cooking and household chores. She was paid three dollars a week. Grandma House thought that entirely too much, and thought a dollar and a half sufficient, but Mommy said, "Now, Ma, that's not very much, she's worth at least three dollars." Mabel described how Mommy would heat irons over the fire, pick one up and quickly rub her apron over the bottom to rid it of ashes. (I've already said that she wasn't the cleanest person in the world.) They then had to iron those white shirts for I never saw a country preacher in a colored shirt. It was as much a part of their attire as the backward collar and robe of a Catholic priest. One night at prayer time, (Stringer was living there also) they all knelt in Mommy's little bedroom-sitting room and Grandma House was in the bed listening to them. Now I happen to know that she was very religious but evidently they weren't praying her kind of prayers for she turned over and told them if Ben House was still living, he would kick them all out. Here she was at death's door and ready to kick two preachers out. And of course, Stringer looked sideways over at Mable, and she almost strangled to keep from laughing. It was at this time that Mabel became disillusioned with preachers. She said Brother Pearson put a few moves on her. He'd say, "My, what a pretty girl you are." She wrote, "He'd have laid up with me in a minute, don't talk to me about old sorry preachers. I wouldn't give them the grease off of a fart." As soon as I read that letter, actually, as soon as I finished that sentence, I called Vic and we both agreed that no way Brother Pearson was flirting with Mabel. She had delusions of grandeur and her ego weighed considerably more than she did. And that was a lot.

When I was a very small child, the four of us lived in a tiny frame house on Johns Lane. It was referred to as The Owl Den. My first memory of that place was a large catalpa tree in the front yard. They bloom early in the spring with lovely white flowers that have brown specks in the center. After six or seven days, they all fall at once, creating the effect of a late spring snowfall in an area the circumference of the tree. Then in late summer the tree is covered with worms that make good fish bait. Next to appear are seedpods which resemble Kentucky Wonder pole beans. Then all the leaves fall and the tree is bare and ugly, while others are resplendent in all their fall finery.

I also remember being spanked by Daddy because he was going somewhere and I wanted to go with him. When I wouldn't stop crying, he switched my legs. He was probably going across the river to drink homebrew and he certainly didn't want a small girl tagging along. Actually, he never wanted any one tagging along.

My parents had run off (eloped) to get married when Mother was nineteen and Dad was eighteen. Mommy Johns was unhappy with that situation and said so in no uncertain terms. She thought that Mother had married beneath her. She had to eat every bad word she had said about him in her later years when she was in such poor health and Mother and Daddy were caring for her. She did have grace enough to admit that she had been wrong about him because he did more for her than some of her own sons.

Mother was one of seven children. I know they were not pampered and spoiled. Eking out a living for a family of that size required the participation of everyone. Mother and Aunt Vina (Viney) were the girls. The boys were Clay, Homer, Roland, Herbert, and Elmer, the baby. The two girls grew up to be well-respected wives and mothers, but the boys all had terrible reputations. Deservedly so. The story was told that David Wilhoite, having been told by his wife that she was walking out to the store remarked, "Well, alright, but if you see a Johns, turn around and come back home."

Mommy Johns was the oldest child born to Benjamin and Martha Jane House. Some of their story is told in the History of Jessamine County, Kentucky:

> "Benjamin, was born June 22, 1840, in Jessamine County and was the son of James and Mary Ball House. Children of that marriage were James, Polly, Daniel; John; Samuel; Benjamin; and Kesiah. The family lived in Washington and Lincoln counties

before settling in Jessamine. John House married Sarah Elizabeth Reynolds July 28, 1856. She, their two infant children and his brother Daniel died of flux (whatever that is) in August of 1859, Grieving, John, along with his brother, Benjamin, joined the Union Army, being mustered into the 20th Kentucky Volunteer Infantry on Jan. 6, 1862. They participated in the battles of Shiloh and Corinth, Miss., and John was present but not actively engaged at the battle of Perryville, their regiment being held in reserve. On July 5, 1863, the 20th Kentucky was guarding the railroad at Lebanon. They were attacked by Confederate Gen. John H. Morgan's Calvary and fought an intensive seven-hour battle. Cpl, John House was killed by shrapnel from a cannon ball while firing from the second story of a hotel. Dr. John C Welch was with him when he died. Cpl. Benjamin House was on the ground, firing from behind the chimney corner of a house. He spied a Confederate soldier crawling toward him along a stone wall and killed him. Benjamin was later wounded, hit in the back of the neck by a mini ball. He always stated that the wound was not fatal because the heavy wool collar on his shirt prevented the ball from passing through his neck. They were forced to surrender. Morgan's men forced them to run the nine miles to Springfield, KY before paroling them. The Union Soldiers walked to Camp Nelson. His brother Sam met Ben House there and they returned to Lebanon with a spring wagon to claim Cpl. John House's body."

Mommy Johns had eleven brothers and sisters. Uncle Alvin, one of her brothers, became a schoolteacher and was one of my mother's teachers. He was as honest as all get out. Once Dad had bought a truckload of tools, furniture, etc. at an auction and Uncle Alvin had driven down to Pollard to see if there was anything he could use. Vic was the cashier and when Uncle Alvin bought about thirty dollars worth of stuff, Vic wrote it down, told Uncle Alvin the total and took the money. He started back home, but returned about fifteen minutes later and said, "Victor, you owe me a dime, you over charged me." Well, Vic didn't want to re-add the whole statement, so he apologized, reached in the box and gave him a dime. A few minutes later, Uncle Alvin returned, handed Vic the dime, and explained that he totaled the items again and he was the one who had made the mistake. The House clan was one of the finest, most respected families in Jessamine County. They were honest, hard working, church going people and it does seem strange that all the uncles had that wild streak that so plagued their wives and their mother.

Poor Mommy Johns was kept in a state of anxiety all her life by some escapade or another of her sorry sons. And they were a sorry lot. Sorry in this instance definitely did not mean regretful or apologetic, although they, on occasion, were sorry if they happened to get caught. As a small child, I didn't think my uncles were sorry. Of course, I didn't know anything about their shenanigans until I was much older. And by then, it was sort of a way of life and the only ones who worried about them were their wives and their mother.

Speaking of getting caught, one of the uncles had been fooling around with a married woman. I won't say which one it was but I will say which one it wasn't. It wasn't Roland. This time. The guilty uncle had driven his truck to Mommy Johns' house and parked it on the road just above the house. The wronged husband was actually out looking for his rival and seeing his truck, decided to vent his anger by shooting out both windows and the windshield. That didn't seem drastic enough so he decided to shoot all the tires. The uncle was hiding behind a closed door and could only peek through the glass upper half as he heard first one tire explode, then another and another until all four tires were as flat as pancakes. This same uncle always ran home to Mommy's cellar when he saw a black cloud because he was afraid of storms and knew he could go into the cellar.

Uncle Roland's first marriage was to Alma Sebastian. Alma was fourteen and a half years of age and he was twenty. Mary Ruth was born two and a half years later. Two months later I made my appearance in the world. Alma, Roland and Mary Ruth lived in a tiny house on Gobbler's Knob. And I don't know why it was called Gobbler's Knob.

Back in those days, women ignored pregnancies as much as possible and worked as hard as they would have normally. During Alma's pregnancy, she was riding a horse to the tobacco field when the horse threw her and she had complications with the delivery. Mary Ruth survived but died when she contracted pneumonia at the age of two and a half. Although Uncle Roland lived to be in his eighties, he never forgot Mary Ruth. He always told my mother, "If I die before you do, see to it that I'm buried beside my baby." He was. They are both buried in the House graveyard on Pollard Road. So is his third wife, Jen. Roland and Alma had one more daughter and named her Esther Jane.

I am two years older than Esther, and she was the sister that I never had. We grew up as across the road neighbors, for Roland and Alma divorced and he and Esther came back to live with Mommy Johns. So the child returning to the nest has been going on for a long time. My two sets of Grandparents lived directly across the road from each other; a distance of about half a city block. Since I practically lived with Granny and Grandad, Esther and I played together almost every day.

She and I tried to smoke a weed called "Life Everlasting", and if we couldn't find that; we rolled up newspapers to resemble a cigarette, and pretended to smoke that. We hid behind Mommy's rocking chair, and when she wasn't looking we would light up. Every night she read God's Revivalist, a bi-monthly publication to which every good Methodist subscribed. She read in a semi-whisper, and since she had ill-fitting dentures, the result was whistling as she read. This, combined with the excitement of pretending to be smoking, sent us into fits of giggling. "You children hush now and what on earth are y'all doing? Don't you know that playing with fire will make you wet the bed?" When she was finished reading, it was time for nightly prayers. "Now children, it's time to pray." The three of us knelt at our chairs while she prayed and prayed and prayed. Then it was time for Esther and me to say our little prayer:

> *Now I lay me down to sleep*
> *I pray the Lord my soul to keep*
> *If I should die before I wake,*
> *I pray the Lord my soul to take.*

If we had had a good day playing, we usually went right to sleep, but occasionally, we fussed and fought, then one of us would get up and get in bed with Mommy. Esther didn't want any other cousin except me to spend the night. Once she put burrs in Betty Johns' hair and they had to be cut out. Betty had beautiful brown curly hair but that wasn't a very flattering haircut. I always stayed over there and played until suddenly I realized the sun was almost below the horizon and time for me to scoot across the road to Granny's house. She always walked out to the hen house to wait for me and just as I called to her to tell her I was on my way, Uncle Roland came out, and in a most serious tone, said, "There's bears in them hollers." Or. "Listen, I thought I heard a panther scream." Now, Pollard is very hilly, so of course there are hollows between every hillside. I never heard of a bear being sighted in that area, but when I was eight or nine, he could send me into fits of terror. I was so scared my feet hardly touched the ground.

Uncle Roland had two nicknames. He was tall and thin and answered to, Stringer or Beans.

I don't remember this next story at all, it probably happened before I was born, but it's been handed down over the years, and deserves to be recorded. One morning, Grandpa Johns saw a tin can on top of his front gatepost. He examined it and found a note inside that read, "Put fifty dollars in this can and leave it in this same place by midnight or your best building will go up in flames." The note was signed "The Nitehawk." Grandpa's brother in law, who was a deputy sheriff and another deputy lay in wait as the appointed hour approached. At midnight, they heard someone at the gate grab the can and run. They pursued, shooting at the thief, but were unable to catch him. They went to Lexington and returned around daybreak with two bloodhounds. The dogs took one sniff at the gate, turned and led the officers to The Nitehawk's house, where the criminal's wife was picking buckshot from his behind. He was sentenced to prison for two years, but after about a year, Grandpa Johns circulated a petition to get him released. The petition was successful and The Nighthawk returned to the community to lead a long and productive life, forever grateful to his benefactor. This story was told over and over at the Sunday afternoon gatherings, and when the narrator got to the part about the bloodhounds, I always climbed into the nearest adult lap. Even the thought of bloodhounds was enough to send me into a state of terror. Esther told me that Mommy kept that note for years. It had matches glued to it for added effect. It was hidden in a closet under the stairs and Esther would get it out and read it.

Often on a Sunday summer afternoon several of the aunts, uncles, and cousins would visit at Mommy's house for a watermelon or mush melon feast or a freezer of Aunt Dallas' homemade banana ice cream. We children climbed to the top of that hill that served as a front yard, and turned somersaults down to the sidewalk. Only we called them summersets. One afternoon Mommy Johns looked at the small children and said, "Poor innocent children, they don't know what troubles life has in store for them." I was quite young when I heard her say that but I've never forgotten the sadness in her voice as she made that statement.

Life certainly had more than a few troubles in store for her. She was the oldest child in that swarm of children that Grandma House bore and I once heard her say, "I raised Ma's children." Grandpa Johns died in 1928 of heart dropsy - known today as congestive heart failure. I asked Vic if he had a long illness and he said that people back in those days had no time for long illnesses. There was too much work to be done.

Mommy was the only person I knew in Pollard who had guinea hens. They are a nervous metallic colored fowl, good for little except ornamentation. They were more adept at flying than the geese and hens, so of course, Esther and I took great delight in chasing them. This was strictly forbidden, but when Mommy was working in some far away field, we felt that what she didn't know wouldn't hurt her. When we were around, they spent most of their time in the treetops. Occasionally, I see a flock of guinea hens and I always think of Mommy and Esther.

My two grandmothers were different in a lot of ways but nowhere was it more apparent than in the way they kept themselves busy. Mommy actually preferred working in the fields to housework. Her hands were never idle, except on Sunday. And they weren't too idle then for she was forever roaming those hillsides and hollers looking for card players and drinking. The commandment, "Remember the Sabbath day and keep it holy" was taken literally. People went to church, ate Sunday dinner and sat outside on the front porch in the summer time or in front of the fireplace in the wintertime. Company was always welcome any time. Often neighbors would get their evening chores finished, get a lantern, and walk a mile or so to "go bed time settin" with friends or neighbors 'round the pike. Remember - no streetlights, and darkness might fall before getting on back down the road. Y'all come.

Quilting and sewing were wintertime activities. During those winter evenings, Esther and I started a nine-patch quilt every year and never finished one of them. But we'd play with those scraps until we heard, "Now, children, it's time to pray." We didn't just bow our heads and pray; we had to kneel by our chairs and no giggling was allowed.

Mommy John's house was larger than Granny and Grandad's. It was situated just below Johns' Lane and built in the middle of a hillside. There were four entrances to that house. A front porch held the inevitable swing and the door opened into the parlor or front room. She had some rather nice furnishings in that room. An oak hall tree with a beveled mirror held hats or coats; her piano graced the wall to the left and a pretty library table sat in front of the back window. (All that stuff was pretty, if you liked oak.) On the left of that room was a bedroom, which was mostly used for company. Going through that room, we entered her little bedroom sitting room, which also had a door that opened to the side porch. This was the door that one of the uncles hid behind while an angry husband was demolishing his truck.

Adjacent to that room was the kitchen. Mommy was not the world's best housekeeper and I always felt that her kitchen would not have passed a health inspection. During the summer months, while they were making jam, canning peaches, etc., flies would be drawn to the kitchen like a tumblebug to a horse pile. Now there was always a yellow sticky fly strip hanging from the ceiling, but it could hold only so many and the fact that there were holes in the screen door didn't help any. So about two times every day we were forced to get a towel and start chasing flies toward the door while a third person held the door open. I became so adept at killing flies with a fly swatter that I could swat them in mid air.

She did have a makeshift sink in the kitchen; I think they were called dry sinks. But she had, without a doubt, the most discolored dishrag I have ever seen. It was black with grease from that old stove and always had a sour smell. But cleanliness was not one of her top priorities. I believe I've already said that once, but that's all right. If she had had a top ten list, number ten would have been to get her sons on the road to heaven and number nine would have been money. I asked Vic what he remembered most about her and he said she was the most frugal person he had ever known.

I asked some of Aunt Vina's girls to share some of their memories and Bernice said she and Mommy hated each other. But I can't imagine Mommy hating any one. It was probably a one sided dislike. One of the twins said she always seemed to be cross and cranky. Wonder why! If I had all those grandchildren living with me, I would have moved out to a motel had there been such an establishment. I never thought of her as being cross or cranky. She often sang while she worked and seemed to wear a smile far more often than Granny. I drifted a bit there, didn't I? But I must write these little side stories down as they come to mind or I'll be sure to forget them. Back to her house.

She had a walnut drop leaf table, which Mother inherited, had refinished, and used as a focal piece in her living room for years. On the left side of the kitchen was the kitchen cupboard, with its pull out biscuit board where she rolled out those marvelous teacakes. We really didn't care if her apron was smudgy or if she had a bit of field dirt under her fingernails. Actually, there was more than a bit. Behind the kitchen was a glassed in back porch that was furnished with a big oak table and chairs, a small cherry wash stand and an oak china cabinet. A door from this room led to a walkway to the smokehouse. Another bedroom joined that back porch and Mommy's bedroom. Located in that room was a lovely Victorian (again, if you liked that stuff) cherry bookcase filled with of Grandpa Johns' books. Esther has the bookcase and my mother was to inherit the books. For some unknown reason, she never got them, and it's just as well, she wouldn't have read them anyway. I hope Esther has them. Upstairs consisted of five rooms. Three were actual bedrooms and two were combination storage and sleeping rooms. One of the bedrooms had a window through which we could crawl out onto the roof of the side porch. If someone would stand and catch us we would jump off the porch. Roland would hold up his arms and tell Aunt Vina's five-year-old Paul to jump and just as he'd bend his legs to fly in the air, Roland would drop his arms. Of course, he wouldn't really let him fall but Paul would start crying.

The cellar was built into the hillside and that was where she kept those wonderful dill pickles. That was also where Uncle Elmer ran to every time he saw a black cloud or heard thunder. Always chewing gum. And always had an extra piece for Esther and me. And I didn't realize it but anyone who has a lick of sense can figure out which uncle hid behind the door when his truck was being shot to smithereens.

Unexpected company was commonplace. Some friend or relative might find themselves a bit ahead in the daily grind of farm chores and decide to go visiting. Since there were no telephones, a call was impossible. People simply came visiting. They didn't just drop in for a cup of coffee and a chat, they spent the day. The hostess had to go to the chicken coop, kill and dress a chicken, and cook a company dinner. The menu, of course, was dependent upon the season. Fried chicken in the summer, pork in the winter and if the company happened to be a favorite relative or a special friend, a trip was made to the smoke house and a shoulder might be sliced and served. They usually sewed or quilted, had a nice visit and forgot about sorry sons and hard times.

Speaking of those quilting B's, I just thought of something funny that Mother wrote to me and I'm sure she also wrote the same story to Aunt Vina. This happened after I had been married for several years. During one of those quilting parties, one Kissin' Ridge housewife was bemoaning the fact that her daughter refused to help her with the quilting. She informed them all, "I won't give her ary a one; she'll not let nary a fart under them." But you can be sure Mother didn't write fart like that; she put a space between each letter, like f-a-r-t. That was to let me know that she wasn't saying that word; she was spelling it. And I might as well tell who said that, too, it was Fannie Taylor, mother of Burl and Henrietta. In fact, I told Burl that I was telling that story and he said that sounds just like her. Granny never used that particular word either. She always said, "Somebody has cracked their credit." She was not referring to a financial situation either. Another strange word Grandad spawned was faunchin. It meant someone was inpatient or angry. Neither Victor nor I ever heard these used by any other family.

Back to quilting. Another quilter's stitches didn't quite come up to Mommy's standards and as soon as the quilting party was over, she always ripped those stitches out and restitched the offending squares. Or at least that is what Esther told me. I find that just a bit hard to believe because I never thought she was that meticulous about anything. She was too busy.

As the company was leaving, the hostess stood in the door and said, "Come." The company replied, "I will, you come." This was a shortened version of "Y'all come back and see us sometime."

I happen to have inherited one of Mommy's quilts. It is a lovely red and white effort called Drunkard's Path. I've always wondered if she knew the name of the pattern, because she was, to say the least, a teetotaler. Although she never stooped so low as Granny, who became so fed up with Daddy's drinking that she found his supply of home brew, poured it out, and filled the bottles with Croton Oil, which was a quick acting cramp producing laxative.

Not only was Mommy Johns a teetotaler, she refused to allow a deck of cards in her house. They were certainly associated with the devil. Not only were they not allowed in her house, they were not allowed on her property. There was an old carriage house, which no longer held buggies or carriages, but had lots of other interesting (to Esther and me) artifacts. Mommy hung all ancient clothing around the walls on ten-penny nails. They were kept out there because her house had only one closet that I can remember. The pockets of those old coats or pants were the perfect place for Roland to keep his playing cards. Well, it was perfect until she found them. She had eyes in the back of her head and a nose like a bloodhound. Often, after Sunday dinner, when she should have been resting or reading, she could be seen walking up and down those hills and hollers, looking for gamblers or moonshiners. One time she was ramblin' around where she had no business because Esther told me she found a still on property that belonged to one of my great uncles. And he wasn't even on her side of the family!

Vic tells me that Roland and his friends played a card game called Pitch, which was similar to bridge. I don't know how he knew that, because he never played bridge in his entire life. But, anyway, they gambled, but not in walking distance of Mommy Johns.

If Esther and I had been especially bad or worrisome, she told us that "Ol' Scratch" would get us if we didn't watch out. That was another name for Satan. Or if we didn't be good girls, we would go to the bad place. Another one of her threats was, "Now, don't make me have to whip you." We thought that was so funny - as if we were likely to make any one whip us. We must have been a nuisance to her, for she was constantly telling one of us that the Booger man was going to get us.

Uncle Clay and Aunt Laura

Mrs. Clay (Laura Wilson) Johns

Mommy's first son, Clay, married Laura Wilson and they were the parents of seven children, Mabel, Jouette, Hershel, Houston, Kenneth and Lloyd. I was unaware until just recently that they had a child who died at a very early age. People of that day and age believed in omens and apparitions. Mommy Johns' house had a glassed in back porch eating area that over looked the orchard. Several members of the family were gathered back there when they saw a white ghost like figure rise from the hill and ascend until out of sight. That night Uncle Clay and Aunt Laura's child died. I'm sure it was a bit of fog coming up out of that holler but to them that was the spirit of that little child ascending into heaven.

They started their married life in Nicholasville. Mabel was their first child and when she entered the first grade her teacher assigned her a seat beside a small girl named Lulu. Childlike, Mable said, "Mama told me not to sit by her." When the teacher asked, "Why not?" Mabel whispered that her mama had said that Lulu had lice. Be that as it may, lice shows no discrimination, Mabel caught them, and swears that her Mother picked seventy-five from her head. (And I know that is a total fabrication.) Mabel grew up to be fat and very pretty. A few years ago she decided that she looked like Liz Taylor. And perhaps she did favor her a bit. Every September, former Pollardites meet for a reunion in the Methodist church then have supper at the recreation building. The first time I went, there sat Mabel with a sixteen-inch high (at least!) white wig on her head and wearing a black dress with considerable cleavage showing. My mother would have absolutely loved seeing that. Mabel can switch from Jekyll to Hyde in the blink of an eye. When I read Mother's diaries, about every third entry referred to Mabel bringing her something from the country. Then when Uncle Herbert died and Aunt Mayme went to the nursing home, James, the executor gave Mother a cupboard. Well, you'd have thought it was brought over on the Mayflower. Mabel called Mother and raved and ranted until Mother hung up on her and they never spoke to each other again. She didn't even come to mother's funeral. But before Mother died she told me she wanted the cupboard sold and half the money was to go to Mabel. Victor and I just laughed and said, "Yeah, right."

Mommy Johns built them a three-room house on Pollard Road; they lived there all their lives. Of course, the house was enlarged as their family increased.

I was never close to these cousins; they were all so much older than I. They lived on a parcel of land that Mommy Johns owned adjacent to

Aunt Minnie and Uncle Larkin. They were a constant source of annoyance to Aunt Minnie and the other neighbors for he had absolutely no pride in the appearance of the property. Surrounding the house were broken down iceboxes, pieces of lumber, axles, fenders, motors, sewing machines and the yard had never felt a lawn mower. Mommy supported that family all her life. Every time Clay came to visit, she went to the smokehouse and took down a shoulder, and then she'd go to the cellar and present him with several jars of beans, peaches, pickles etc. One of his children told my mother that they would have starved had it not been for Mommy. The other children were aware of this situation, but they felt no animosity toward him, or if they did, I was unaware of it. Not only did Mommy contribute to their support, the brothers and sisters took them food and several entries in mother's diaries referred to giving Clay five or ten dollars. Even Herbert gave them money now and then, according to letters written to Aunt Vina from my mother. I'd have to see that to believe it, but I know my mother would not have said it had it not been true.

There was some reference to heart trouble in his early years of marriage and perhaps, because of that, he was reluctant to work. That's really being too kind, for he was hound dog lazy and dirt sorry. There was a sawmill on the place and he occasionally sawed a load of lumber. He was a genius in the way of mechanics, and could repair any car or truck. Or any other appliance, after other appliances became commonplace.

Like most everyone else in Pollard, he had a very low opinion of Franklin Roosevelt. Commenting on one of FDR's fireside talks Clay said, "He's lyin' and I wish that he knowed that I know that he's lyin.' "

Great Uncle Cy Teater and Aunt Laura Belle had purchased a nineteen thirty-two Dodge. All went well for a few weeks, until a strange and unusual noise surely promised future trouble. The car was promptly parked in the barn. Country folks who were affluent enough to own a car parked it in the barn. After all, if it was good enough for the horse; it was good enough for the car. Although Mommy and Grandpa Johns owned a car and had a garage built for it. That was another place where Esther and I smoked, under the garage.

Anyway, Daddy knew a golden opportunity when he saw one so he bought the car for thirty-five dollars and Uncle Cy and Aunt Laura Belle reverted to a more trusted means of transportation - a horse and buggy. Dad drove the car to Clay's house and kept the engine running. Now, Clay had a habit of grabbing his shirtfront with two fingers, shrugging his shoulders, and then spitting. So when Dad asked him what was wrong with the car, Clay went through that ritual, listened to the engine for a few minutes, repeated the process, and then told him exactly what was needed in the way of repairs. And repaired it. (Cars and trucks of that era had no left turn or right turn hand signals. To turn right the driver rolled the window down and stuck the arm straight up in the air. Straight down meant, stop. Straight out meant left or checking to see if it's raining or looking at those cows over yonder in that pasture.)

It was a standing joke with my Mother that Clay was simply unable to talk to a woman without touching her on the arm, although to my way of thinking that was much better than touching her in some other places. Mabel once told him to stop doing that for the women didn't like it and he said "Shucks! They do too!" Another Johns man who thought he was God's gift to womankind. But back in those days, a married man wasn't supposed to look at a woman other than his wife, and if he did, she wasn't supposed to return the look and to touch another female was unthinkable. In fact there just wasn't any public hugging goin' on. And hardly any touching.

All of these cousins married except Kenneth who wasn't quite right. He was just about a half a bubble off plumb. They all had children except Jouette who adopted a small girl and called her Pard.

Uncle Clay survived Aunt Laura by many years, he was "way up there" when he died. And wherever he is, he is probably grabbing his shirtfront, shrugging, spitting, and asking if it's hittin' on all eight. And, in his spare time, touching some female on the arm.

Aunt Vina and Uncle Harry

Golden Wedding Anniversary Noted

Approximately 150 guests called on Rev. and Mrs. H. H. Davis of Springdale last Sunday afternoon when the couple observed their 50th wedding anniversary. Included were all of the couple's 10 children, the first time all the family had been together in 25 years. The couple is shown here shortly before the anniversary cake was cut for the open house reception held from 2 to 5 p.m. (Ray Watson photo)

Uncle Harry and Aunt Vina Davis

Mommy Johns' first daughter was Aunt Vina. Called Viney. She and

Mother were very close, as befitted the only two girls in that swarm of boys. When she had completed as much schooling as the local school system offered, she was sent to Kingswood College for the purpose of furthering her education and also because Grandpa Johns wanted her to distance herself from one of the local swains. I recently learned that she and Grandad's brother, Uncle Henry were, as they said back then, settin' out. I don't know why he had a problem with Uncle Henry for he went to dental school and became a very successful dentist. I never have understood how she could enroll in Kingswood College, when she never went to High School. But be that as it may, she found more than an education at Kingswood, for Harry Davis was also enrolled there. He took one look, and decided then and there that he was going to marry that girl. And he did. Or so the story goes. During her second year, they borrowed a buggy from some farmer and as they said back in those days, ran off and got married. Uncle Harry became a Nazarene preacher and when asked why he chose, or was chosen by, as the case may be, the Nazarenes he explained that no other denomination was devout enough for him.

Once, in the late fifties, she and I happened to be visiting Pollard at the same time. I had four stair-step children, and she said, "Gwen, honey, you're just like I was. My husband was no pig, but every time he touched me, I had a baby." (I kept thinking of that, "Gwen, honey, you're just like I was" - eleven children! So Bill had a vasectomy.) Once, he must have touched her two times, because she had twin girls, Ruth and Esther. She had 11 children in fourteen years. Their children were Virginia, Evangeline, Ruth and Esther, Gene, Paul, Bill, Morrison, Lucille, Bernice and Mildred. But every time she was blessed with another child, she loved it with all her heart.

One of the most rewarding things about this writing is that I have begun a correspondence with some of my Davis cousins. I started writing to the twins and have learned quite a bit about their home life.

Ruth and Esther Davis

Every night, before bedtime they had family prayers and Aunt Vina read a few chapters from the Bible. Then one or the other would talk about hell - how terribly hot it is - how it goes on forever and ever and ever. All this frightened the twins so as to bring on innumerable attacks of diarrhea. Aunt Vina and Uncle Harry were very loving parents, but truly believed that fright was the most effective way to teach a child right from wrong. Each child was required to say a prayer. Ruth said the same prayer every night. One night she decided to break the monotony and launched into a lengthy devotion, until Uncle Harry interrupted with a "Pray right, Ruth!" Bill always said, "Jesus wept." Finally, one night, Uncle Harry said, "Bill, tomorrow night, say a new scripture." The next night, Bill's scripture was, "Behold we put bits in the horse's mouth that they should obey us."

The twins were a hoot. One night, during one of those innumerable revivals, they dressed Paul, the youngest child, in a pink dress that belonged to Lucille, and then sent him over to sit with the three older girls. I know that Aunt Viney laughed about that because she had a great sense of humor and could always find something to smile about. Even she could not tell them apart. When one got in trouble she switched both. On another night, the altar call had gone on for hours (Just one more last stanza) and when Aunt Vina arrived home with her brood, they started the evening prayers, but they were missing one child. Paul had curled up on a church pew and was sound asleep.

I can't imagine having to care for a family that large. Especially with an invalid husband. When he was thirty-four, he was very ill with T.B. in both kidneys. The doctors removed one kidney and told him and Aunt Vina that he only had about six months to live. What did they know! He lived many more years to glorify God.

During the mid-thirties, Uncle Harry had somehow managed to accumulate $500.00. He decided to invest in an oil well. Oil was very profitable for many Oklahomans, but not for him. He went broke. They had absolutely nothing, so what was there to do except come to Pollard and spend the summer with Mommy Johns. Fortunately, the house was large, with three bedrooms downstairs, and the entire upstairs was converted into a sleeping area. There was no bathroom problem for the house had no bathroom.

That was one summer that I had a whole gaggle of cousins to play with. Bernice was a bit older, Lucille a year or two younger, and although Gene was about three years older, he was my constant companion that summer. We even favored each other. He had as many freckles as I and our hair was practically the same color. But he was a lot sneakier than I ever dreamed of being. If one of her children had done something that warranted a punishment, Aunt Vina always sent the offender to cut his own switch. Gene taught the others how to cut a notch or two in the switch so after a lick or two the switch would break in two.

I was such a tomboy; I wanted to do everything he did. If he climbed a tree, I climbed a tree, if he jumped out of the barn loft, so did I. If he walked to the river, I was right behind him. One night, a half dozen of us were piled on Mommy's bed and Gene leaned over and whispered something in Bernice's ear and I knew he said something snotty about me and she later told me that he had said "Gwen is so ugly she's cute." I still followed him everywhere.

Since one of Aunt Vina's twins was named Esther and was eighteen or so, we had two Esther's that summer. So we called them Big Esther and Little Esther.

Poor little Esther had a hard row to hoe that summer. She was accustomed to being the center of attention and was jealous of any other grandchild except me. I posed no threat to her serenity, for I was so close to the Grandparents across the road. I'm sure that summer was a difficult time for everyone. Aunt Vina's children were completely out of their element, for they had lived in a not quite so rural environment. I know they laughed at our accents. One idiom they thought particularly funny was our referring to someone living "just around the pike a piece."

Uncle Harry was a good man, but was practically useless on a farm, because of poor health.

Fortunately food on a farm was no problem. Everyone pitched in, canned the abundant produce, neighbors had showers for them, giving them anything they could spare and when time came for them to return to Arkansas, Uncle Elmer loaded everything, plus a few relatives who wanted the adventure of a trip to Arkansas, on his truck. The family was loaded in Uncle Harry's car and prior to departure; Mommy

Johns came forth with the basis for one of Victor's all time favorite stories and mine. She was pure Appalachian, (Vic says Old English) said "hit" for it, "hain't" for ain't (much to the disdain of the across the road Grandmother.) Mommy walked up the hill, where they were all loaded in Uncle Harry's car, gave him $300 which was a monumental sum in those days, and said to him, "Now, (Sniff), don't tithe on this, hit's been tithed on."

A true Christian, in those days, gave ten percent of everything he earned to the church, and she knew that Uncle Harry would surely do so. He did recuperate, financially, (with the help of Mommy Johns) and managed to buy twenty-five acres of land outside of Springdale, Arkansas. One summer Roland was out there helping them set out a strawberry patch, and he said, "Harry, do you prop this plant up with two rocks or three?" That was his opinion of Arkansas soil. Esther told me that when any of the uncles would come for a visit, Mommy would always make them give her fifty cents or a dollar to send to Aunt Vina. "Times are awful hard for them right now and you can spare a little."

In later years, Uncle Harry discovered that man cannot live by religion alone and became a very successful builder. I am sure he still tithed. He was a kind and gentle man who never raised his voice in reproach and I loved being around him. He was not the only uncle who loved us children, but his love was shown in a different way. Some completely ignored us, some "aggervated" us, but Uncle Harry always told us stories. Some were Bible stories, most all had a moral; he was a good man who made me want to be good, too. Although, after he had gone back to Arkansas, Esther and I were usually back under some out building smoking Life Everlasting or chasing guineas.

It was about this time that Mommy let Esther and me have the use of one of her corn cribs. Her farm had several outbuildings. There was a garage for the car that Grandpa Johns had before he died (and willed to "My wife Cordie" - for what, I don't know because she never drove a car in her life), the old carriage house where Roland hid his cards, and the barn where we jumped out of the barn loft, the smoke house, and an unused corn crib. Dad attended many auctions. Once, he drove up, parked the truck, got out and unloaded a tiny table and two chairs, a doll bed and dresser and a real miniature cast iron stove that had been a salesman's sample. It actually had a stovepipe. I had never seen anything so beautiful. We could build a fire in it; fill the little reservoir with water and our house was elegantly furnished. We borrowed (I say borrowed; actually we sneaked them out) Mommy's embroidered pillowslips for sheets for the doll bed, and used her best tea towels for a tablecloth. Of course, her best tea towels were made from flour sacks.

Prior to that, we had pretended, but now we could really cook. We filled the tiny reservoir with water so we had hot water to use for dish washing. About one fourth cup of pinto beans had been set to soak in the little bean pot the previous night. When Mommy mixed the cornbread batter for dinner she gave us a half-cupful. While the beans cooked, we fried hoecakes on the tiny griddle, scrambled an egg in the small skillet, and then invited our guests to join us. Uncle Harry and another preacher, Brother Pearson, came to Pollard for the purpose of conducting summer time revivals. Of course, they stayed at Mommy Johns and this meant four more for her to feed. Esther and I invited them to our "house" for dinner and they pretended to sit on the tiny chairs, asked the blessing and ate from the doll dishes. In retrospect, I can't believe Mommy actually let us use that building to build a fire and cook. One had to be so careful of fires for there was no fire department and once a house or barn caught fire there was nothing to be done, but we were very careful.

Now here was a Nazarene preacher holding a revival in a Methodist church. This probably wouldn't happen today. But people in those days did almost anything to earn a quarter or even a dime. It was said that Uncle Harry wasn't a very good preacher and now I know why. Pollard folks liked their religion LOUD and he wasn't a yeller. Like Brother Willie Peel.

Aunt Viney wrote to Mother every week, but her penmanship was so poor as to be almost illegible. This was a result of a lack of time, for she believed that idle hands were the devil's workshop. She made throws or quilts on her sewing machine; these were based on the crazy quilt pattern. Since I sewed constantly for our girls, I sent left over fabric to her. I sure didn't want to make a quilt. She made one each for Robin, Cherry and Carol Ann. It was fun to look them over and point out the brown plaid polyester from which I had made a skirt and vest for Robin, and there was the ice blue satin piece left over from Cherry's two piece pants suit with the rhinestone buttons and the marabou feather trim. And look, here was the yellow organdy remnant from Carol Ann's Easter dress. Cotton, satin, wool, corduroy, small pieces, large pieces, it made no difference; nothing was wasted for she was a product of that waste not want not generation.

It's always been a source of amazement to me that Mommy Johns, who was widowed at an early age, was financially able to be of assistance to so many of her children. But somehow, she always had money. She sold eggs, chickens, and cream. Every fall, she and the boys killed several hogs and she sold most of the hams, while the family ate the shoulders, backbone, and sausage. Country ham was a great delicacy for city folks and while shoulders were good and had the same flavor, they were much tougher than hams.

Only one of the Davis boys is still living. Morrison was a casualty of World War Two, Bill died of cancer and a drunken driver killed Gene.

Uncle Roland

Roland, nicknamed Beans or Stringer (he answered to either) was Victor's and my favorite uncle, even if he did keep me in a constant state of fear by telling me that there were bears and panthers in "them hollers."

He was a tall, skinny long legged man who could eat six meals a day. When people wondered why he stayed so skinny (unlike Uncle Homer and Uncle Herbert) he always said I eat so much, it makes me pore to carry it. And it about did.

Uncle Roland and Victor - 1925

He married Alma Sebastian when she was fourteen. They moved into a small house on Gobbler's Knob, owned by Mommy Johns and two years later Mary Ruth was born. She was a beautiful child but like so many others at that time, her days were short on this earth and she died of pneumonia at the age of two and a half. Two years later, another daughter, Esther, was born, but by that time the marriage was beginning to deteriorate and something rare for that time occurred. They were divorced.

After he and Alma divorced, he married a woman named Gertrude Lowery. That marriage was of short duration, for Gertrude died soon thereafter.

He had a remarkable memory, and even when he was in his seventies, could recall events that had taken place as far back as the twenties. He could also remember the day of the week on which these events occurred. He also knew the Bible backward and forward and could find a verse to suit any occasion. This ability served him well in later years when asked by Victor if he was having an affair with a neighborhood - married woman. Of course, Vic knew he was, for everyone in Pollard was buzzing with gossip and Dad had already informed him of the rumor. Never one to be content with rumor less than fact, Vic approached him about the woman in question. When Roland started quoting some Bible verse about when a man can't take care of his own wife, Vic said, "That's all I want to know." and turned and walked away.

All this brings to mind a funny story about Roland and this same woman. They had been chasing each other for quite some time and I don't know which one caught the other, but it really doesn't matter. And there's no point in being so secretive about it, her name was Jen Hay, she was married to a man named Early, and they lived just "down the pike a piece." They're all dead now, anyway.

Roland had the reputation of liking watermelon better than any food on this earth. So one Wednesday night, after prayer meeting, he invited Jen and Early down to Mommy's for some watermelon. One of the other uncles happened to be visiting and by this time, he also had his suspicions about Roland and Jen. He later told Vic that he knew all the rumors were true when he saw Roland cut out the heart of that watermelon and hand it to Jen. Now, we all know that the center of the watermelon is the sweetest and most succulent, and is almost completely without seeds. And for Roland to share the heart of the watermelon there had to be some hanky-panky going on. And there was. Early divorced Jen and she and Roland lived together for many years in what was then called a common-law marriage. Later, when he told her what the other uncle had said, she laughed and said, "What you don't know is that he was after me too." See what I mean about Mommy's sorry sons? As the old saying goes, he bit off more than he could chew when he finally married her, for I think the honeymoon was over before the ink on the marriage license was dry. I could never think of her as an aunt.

It's beyond me what either one of them saw in her, for she was a short dumpy woman who had already had several children. She smeared, and I do mean smeared, her lips with the brightest red lipstick available. Any kind of make-up was called paint. Lip liner had yet to appear in the cosmetic counter so the "paint" spread upwards, downwards and sideways through the wrinkles around her mouth until her lips looked like a possum's hind end in pokeberry time and by no stretch of the imagination could she have been called attractive.

All this was a heavy burden on Mommy, for Roland had lived with her so many years that she felt they were a family unit. In fact, she even told one of her grandchildren that Jen was breaking up her home.

Roland had an insatiable appetite. We often teased him and told him he probably had a tapeworm. One of his favorite evening meals was a glass of buttermilk and corn bread. There was always left over corn bread from the noon meal and this was broken up and crumbled into the buttermilk. If buttermilk was unavailable, sweet milk was used. This was called crumble-in. (Hey, I'll bet those left over hush puppies from Willow Pond Catfish restaurant would be good crumbled up in a cold glass of buttermilk.) Crumble-in was never eaten from a bowl; it was always eaten from a glass and Roland was the only person I ever knew who could eat it from the blade of a knife and never waste a crumb or drop. Esther and I watched him, wondering when he would slice his tongue half in two; we couldn't understand why he did that, as Mommy had plenty of spoons. Roland also ate crumble-in with a fork. Speaking of strange food habits, Mommy Johns would often eat a cold biscuit with ice cream. Of course, she preferred teacakes or some other kind of cake but she couldn't eat ice cream without something to accompany it.

Roland had a dry wit and often said some very funny things. Bernice wrote about a visit that she and Aunt Vina made to Kentucky after Uncle Harry died. Aunt Vina felt a deep need to see her sister and her brothers. By this time, both sisters were widows and Mother had bought a house in town. She cooked a "field hand" dinner and invited the brothers, Aunt Mayme, and Mayme's sister Lulu. As usual, the conversation centered on crops, money and death. Uncle Homer remarked that Ol' Man Peel, who lived down yonder on the river, had died last night. Herbert, always thinking of money, said, "Wonder what he left?" Roland thought for a few seconds, and then said, "Everything."

He was never happier than when he was teasing some child. Well, maybe when he was chasing Jen. But picking on kids ran a close second. He was also very happy when he was eating. The summer that the Davis clan was there, his primary target was Aunt Vina's six-year-old Paul. He started kidding that child about sucking eggs. Of course, poor Paul cried and denied such a despicable act. One night at the supper table Roland had placed some egg shells in Paul's chair and the resulting crunch when that small bottom met the chair seat sent Roland into gales of laughter and finger pointing accusations. Some adults delighted in teasing children. Many a two year old thought his nose was gone forever when an adult pinched it with thumb and fore finger while quickly sticking the thumb between his middle finger and fore finger and exclaiming, "I gotcha nose!" I was firmly convinced that swallowing a watermelon seed would result in a watermelon vine growing out my nose. Being teased - actually, we called it being aggervated - got me in a peck of trouble when I was about four or five. Holly Hurt was aggervating me about something and I must have had a short fuse that day and I called him a bastard. I had no idea what that word meant or where I heard it but I soon learned that it was a bad word. My next memory was being seated on the kitchen table at grannies' house while three grown-ups gave me a talking to. Grandad said nothing for he knew that Granny could say enough for everyone. I didn't get a spanking; I'm sure they all realized that I was unaware of the meaning of that word. I do remember Vic standing in the door grinning from ear to ear. He probably tattled on me.

Vic and Roland were very close, in fact after Daddy died; Roland was more or less a surrogate father. Vic's son-in-law, Charles is highly educated, has a degree in nuclear physics and then became an anesthesiologist but still enjoyed a visit to Pollard and a chat with Roland. Roland was also highly educated, but by life, not books.

Uncle Homer and Aunt Hazel

Uncle Homer married Hazel Carter. They lived in the Loganna community and were the parents of three children. William Allen was their first son. Next came the twins, Betty and Bobby. Victor thinks Homer was one of the funniest men he has ever known and indeed there are some funny stories about him.

Homer Johns (seated) and Calvin Comley - 1917

Most people in those days somehow managed to scrape together enough money to buy a small insurance policy. Uncle Homer was no exception. He had a small health and accident policy and when he had an accident of some kind he, of course, filed a claim. For some reason his insurance company refused to honor the claim and Uncle Homer sat down and fired off a letter, informing them that they should be ashamed "trying to cheat ignorant people like me." Sometimes I wonder if that might have come from that endless supply of Victor's stories and his gift for using the right victim in the right story. But he swears that one is true.

One of Homer's shenanigans is the topic of another of Victor's and my favorite stories. (And we know this is true.) Uncle Homer had a bad habit of picking his nose during stressful situations. Since we lived in a rural area and did not have access to a Kroger store, there was a Donaldson Bakery Company that provided delivery service to country stores. Such stores in our area were the L.D. Fain store, the Mount Lebanon store and of course, Reynolds' store. The Donaldson Bakery Co. delivered light bread, small cakes and breakfast rolls to all three general stores.

When Homer was a young man, he was accused of fathering an out of wedlock child. Of course, he denied the accusation, but the mother of the child filed a paternity suit. After repeated denials, and continued accusations by her attorney, he finally squirmed around in the witness chair, stuck his finger up his nose and said, "Well, hit hain't mine, hit belongs to that Donaldson Bread man."

He was tall, dark, swarthy and became very heavy. By heavy, I mean about 260 pounds. One summer Sunday afternoon he and Aunt Hazel had come to visit Mommy Johns and decided to walk across the road and visit with us and perhaps have a bowl of leftover ice cream. The men sat on the front porch smoking cigarettes and flipping the butts out in the yard. Chickens were supposed to stick to their own territory, but they were very adept at getting over or under a fence and as soon as they saw that cigarette butt hit the ground, there they were ready to pounce-fire and all. So they did. Talk about jumping and jerking. But even a chicken had some sense. Once burned, they'd follow the arching white object to the ground, and then walk off. Tobacco was hazardous to their health, also. I'll say it again. Entertainment was scarce.

On our front porch was the usual assortment of metal and kitchen chairs that had been rared back in so many times that the back legs were at least an inch shorter than the front. And of course, the swing. Everyone who had a front porch had a swing. Except Aunt Minnie and Uncle Larkin; they had a glider. But Uncle Homer sat down on one of those old-timey metal chairs that eased up and down, only with Homer as its occupant; it could go nowhere but down and down and down. All the way to the porch floor. That one was told and exaggerated until someone said a forklift was needed to get him up off the floor. Speaking of exaggeration, it was told that a feather could start out in Pollard and by the time it blew into Nicholasville, it had become a full-grown goose.

Homer and one of Uncle Clay's boys were big drinking buddies. At a Lexington beer joint, they were already about three thirds drunk when a waitress walked past their table and Homer said, honey, lets me and you waltz. She wasn't in a waltzing mood and whacked him on the side of the head with an unopened beer bottle. Again he was on the floor but this time out like a light. His shirt popped open and since he hadn't worn an undershirt, Houston said he looked for all the world like a big scraped hog.

In later years, he somehow became involved with some far out religious group, (that meant it wasn't Methodist) and Mother and Aunt Dallas and Aunt Vina were trying to pray him out of that one and put him where they thought he oughta belong. Now here he had quit layin' out, quit drinking, got religion and those women still weren't happy. He couldn't do anything right.

He was in his mid seventies when he died and Aunt Hazel out lived him by several years. My cousin, Wayne, who is a lay preacher, conducted her funeral services.

Uncle Herbert and Aunt Mayme

Herbert and Mayme Johns - 1917

These two were married shortly before Mother and Daddy eloped, and their union produced no children. Aunt Mayme was a schoolteacher and Uncle Herbert was a builder, contractor and part time crook. I always liked Aunt Mayme although I felt she was a bit spacey. She was a short little woman, not much over four feet tall and would have mortgaged the house to have been eight inches taller. She was a good cook and enjoyed having relatives in for Saturday dinner. Her favorite menu always included country ham, (and she might throw in a few country fried steaks and baked chicken) macaroni and cheese and a big pot of cabbage. (Two whites don't make a wrong when Aunt Mayme served them.) She enjoyed cooking so much, that when Bill and I decided to get married, or, as he says, when I decided to get married, Aunt Mayme volunteered to entertain Bill's out of town relatives with the rehearsal dinner. You can bet she didn't have macaroni and cheese that evening; it was country ham and all the trimmings.

Uncle Herbert was the only one of the Johns boys who made a goodly amount of money. He wasn't too particular about how he earned it, either.

They had a nice home in Nicholasville surrounded by several acres. Although he was very selective about it, he believed in sharing his wealth. One of his girlfriends also had a nice home. He told Aunt Vina's twins that he would buy them a bicycle. It's a good thing they didn't hold their breath 'til they got it. One of Vic's daughters said if she'd sit on his lap and blow in his ear he'd give her anything, but she never wanted money that badly.

He was never one of my favorite uncles, although he should have been because after he died, Mother inherited a substantial sum from his estate and this in turn, was passed on to Victor and me.

Aunt Mayme had a widowed sister, Lula Crutchfield, who lived with them as much as she could get by with. Occasionally, she moved out and had her own apartment for a year or so, but before long she moved back in with them. She worked for the telephone company for years and was the "Central" to whom we gave the phone number we wished to have rung.

Uncle Herbert was no exception to the rule when it came to "running around" on his wife. He was seeing some skinny ol' gal in Lancaster and when Aunt Mayme lit into him about it he simply laughed and made some remark about "The closer the bone, the sweeter the meat." He also had one steady in Nicholasville, and when he died he left her a house or two and a Cadillac.

Like all the Johns boys, he was fairly nice looking as a young man, but he definitely did not improve with age. He was a tall, overweight, blustery old windbag with an inflated ego and at the drop of a hat, would start boasting of his accomplishments which were impressive. He built many houses in Nicholasville and also paved several area roads.

His face seemed to sag and melt with age and the wide gash under his nose that served as a mouth was incomplete without a cigar stub in one corner and tobacco juice in the other. His turned up nose was totally devoid of cartilage, and I was always grateful that none of our children favored him. That's another old country saying in which the word favored is substituted for the word resemble, "takes after" is another, as in, Robin takes after her daddy. I later learned that this feature could not be passed on down the line, for his nose was smashed when he was in the act of changing a tire and the rim flew off and hit him in the face.

He did have redeeming qualities though for when Vic and Geraldine were building their first house, he offered the use of any of his equipment or manpower. (My own personal opinion of that is Vic would have had to pay for it.) And even though they were childless, they quite often welcomed a country niece or nephew who needed a place to stay while attending high school. The summer that Aunt Viney brought her family to Pollard, one of the twins lived with them and attended summer school. Morrison, another one of the Davis children also lived with them while attending high school. Victor lived with them during his freshman year. And of course Aunt Mayme's widowed sister and her son James Letcher were there all the time. But that was the custom in those days.

Since Aunt Mayme was a county schoolteacher, arriving home later than Victor, one of his duties was to build a fire when he came home. One afternoon, he was trying to get the fire started and Lulu's twelve-year-old son, James Letcher, continually blew out the match. Vic finally flailed the pee out of him and got the fire built. Herbert thought it was very funny but Mayme and Lulu were upset for days.

In his later years, Uncle Herbert learned to like vodka and seldom sat down to an evening meal in a state of sobriety. To keep Aunt Mayme unaware of his condition, as soon as he came home, he went straight to the bathroom and gargled with mouthwash.

When Daddy "lay a corpse" (I'm really into old country sayings tonight, and although this one is rather self-explanatory, it actually means lying in state at the funeral home) neighbors and friends brought food to Vic and Geraldine's house. Relatives gathered there to have a bite to eat and to comfort and be comforted. Roland and Jen stopped by and so did Herbert, who was, as usual, about three thirds. As was his custom, he went to the bathroom and finding no mouthwash, picked up a bottle of cologne and took a hefty swig. Gen, who didn't know he was in there, opened the door, took one look, backed out and told Missy that Herbert was in there drinking "Colgeen."

Both of them lived long lives. I can't say long happy lives, for he and Mayme and Lulu fought and argued constantly. He preceded her in death by about six years.

Her physical and mental condition deteriorated over the next few years and she became quite careless about her appearance. She had always been somewhat bow-legged and later developed Paget's disease, which only added to the problem. She couldn't cross her legs; in fact, she couldn't even keep them together. And you didn't dare sit across the room from her for just as sure as God made little green apples, you'd get your picture taken.

It became more and more apparent that she was unable to care for herself and since she had no other recourse had to live in a nursing home. During my trips to Nicholasville Mother and I always went to see her and Aunt Minnie, who had taken up residence in the same place. Aunt Mayme was always happy to see us and told us she was going home tomorrow, provided it was not raining, because she needed to get her Christmas shopping done. Some months later, it dawned on her that that was where she was going to spend the remainder of her days, then she always told us, "What a nice place this is, they let me live here and don't charge me anything."

Uncle Elmer and Aunt Dallas

Uncle Elmer was the youngest of the Johns children and was always thought of as the baby of the family. He married Dallas Reynolds and while I always liked him, I thought she was a saint. Her quiet soft voice always had a smile and I never heard it raised in reproach. She was not a pretty woman, but the old cliché -pretty is as pretty does - definitely applied to her.

They had three boys, Wayne, Billy Joe and David. Their first home was a small house down on Gobbler's Knob (now known as just a ways off John's Lane.) That was where I first tasted that delicious banana ice cream that only she could make.

Elmer, Dallas and Wayne Johns

Uncle Elmer was a good-looking man who had sandy red hair; so of course, his nickname was "Red." They had been married for several years before having children, then Wayne was born, about six years later came Billy Joe and after another six years, David was born.

I was twelve or so when Wayne was born and I thought he was the most wonderful baby I had ever known. Actually, he was the only baby I'd ever known. They had moved from Gobbler's Knob to just down the road a piece from us. (That means about a block and a half.) I would have lived with them just to be allowed to hold Wayne. I like to think I was of some help to her, for I remember washing dishes, sweeping floors and any other chores she asked of me.

Aunt Dallas was very religious but not piously obnoxious. In her own quiet way, she was kind to everyone and every night before going to sleep, she re-ran the day's activities in her mind. If she thought she had said or done anything offensive to anyone she wanted to ask for forgiveness. I never heard her say an unkind word, even though she was the wife of one of those Johns men and Lord knows, that would try the patience of Job.

She played the piano and Mother thought I might like to take lessons. Well, that's what she thought, but not what I thought. So when I whined a few times about not having a piano of our own to practice on, she let me stop. Of course, I could have practiced at Mommy's house but she really didn't cotton to the idea of children messing around in her front room. I never really understood what those front rooms were used for. There wasn't a comfortable piece of furniture in there and I can't remember company ever being entertained. I finally decided that was just for show and also the only place they had to keep their dead before burial services.

Uncle Elmer was driving home from Harrodsburg one day, when he suddenly pulled his truck over in Syvella Burgan Robert's yard. He got out, managed to walk to the shade of a big oak tree, where he fell to the ground and started praying to the Lord for help. It was too late and that is where he breathed his last. It was such a shock to everyone and especially to Aunt Dallas and now the soft voice no longer smiled.

It wept.

Many years later, Wayne became a lay preacher. He was always so good he usurped Gene as my favorite cousin and besides that, I always remembered taking care of him when he was a baby. He married a girl named Ruth and when Aunt Dallas became ill with cancer he and Ruth took care of her until she died. He presided at her funeral (which must have been very difficult for him to do.) He asked if anyone would like to say a few words and Uncle Roland stood and said, "She was more like a sister to me than a sister in law." Roy B. Miller said a few words then added, "She was my first teacher." Wayne began his eulogy by saying, "She was my first teacher, too." And more than a few people wept.

Pollard and Some of Its Residents

Uncle Larkin Fain and Uncle Ira Fain

Pollard is hilly, rugged and scenic. Families who have called it home include: Fains, Reynolds, Stinnetts, Millers, Johns, Lockers, Comleys, Hagers, Sebastians, Peels, Mackeys, Wylies, Trues, Houses and Taylors. The store that Milford owned, was operated first by Monroe Miller, then by Garland Reynolds and finally by Roscoe Mackey. It closed about ten years ago. My cousin Wayne inherited it and having no wish to become a country storekeeper, donated it to a fire department and it was used as a demo fire.

In the early 1930's, there was a blacksmith shop and a gristmill both of which were operated by my daddy.

Kissing Ridge is a section of Pollard that got its name from a statement by Kess Burgin. It seems that Bob Wylie's pretty daughters liked to party and play spin the plate. Kess Burgin remarked, there sure is a lot of kissing goin' on on this ridge.

Granny B was one of the oldest residents of Pollard. She was not related to us. Some older men were called Uncle, just as some older women were called Aunt. Occasionally, an older man was called "Old Man" For example Aunt Dallas' father was called "Old Man Joe Reynolds." But not by me. I called him Mr. Reynolds. When Esther, Betty Fain and I were very young, he gave each of us a small white leather Bible. Betty was one of his grandchildren. He and his wife, Ellenor ("Aunt Leanor") were the parents of Garland, Aunt Annie, Aunt Dallas, and Mary. When Garland married Virginia Mackey; they lived with his parents in a big white house very near the store.

Mommie Johns, Aunt Annie Fain, Aunt Leanor Reynolds and Wayne Johns

Every warm sunny day, Mr. Reynolds could be seen sitting out on the front porch in a straight-backed kitchen chair. He suffered from arthritis, was paralyzed from the waist down and his legs conformed to the shape of the chair. He was able to mobilize himself throughout the house by using his shoulders and hands and creating a walking movement with the chair. He was very religious and enjoyed going to church after Carl Bruner, who was handy with a hammer and saw, built and attached a seat to a small red wagon. Mr. Reynolds was lifted onto the wagon, and someone pulled him the half-mile to the church.

Several people in Pollard used what we called "by-words." Meaning they prefaced almost every sentence with a certain word. Mr. Reynolds usually said "Actually" before every sentence. Grandad usually said "Ay." Uncle Wilbert always said "Sy." Arn Burton always said "Pshaw." I suppose that was the equivalent of today's "You know." Y' know.

Granny B lived directly across the road from the schoolhouse, and as such a central resident had many visitors. When Mother and I walked to Mommy Johns, we sometimes stopped to rest and she and Mother would have a nice chat, but not before she went to her kitchen to get a ho-cake for me to eat. A ho-cake is corn pone made without egg and soda. I can't believe I ate that.

Granny "B" Hager
Sept. 11, 1863 — Dec. 31, 1943

Granny B smoked a clay pipe. She was the only female that I knew who used tobacco. I learned many years later that Aunt Laura Johns smoked all her life and of course, Mother said that was what killed her. But somehow, an old lady smoking a clay pipe was acceptable behavior, whereas a young lady who smoked a cigarette was not only a trollop and an object of ridicule, but was headed straight for the depths of Hell. But Granny B sat in her rocking chair, smoking her clay pipe and speaking words of wisdom. When she heard that a local young lady was having an affair, and I'm fairly sure it was with one of the Johns boys, she remembered that the young lady's mother had also been a rounder. She took a puff on her pipe, rocked a few times, and said, "If the mare paces, the colt will pace." Meaning that the young lady's mother had also been around the block a time or two.

Granny B had two husbands. The first one was named Hocker Hager and was accidentally shot one dark night by Burl Taylor's great uncle, who said, "I have killed the best friend I ever had." He left Pollard and lived in Texas the remainder of his life. However, Mr. Hager did not die immediately, and while on his deathbed, asked her never to marry again. She looked him straight in the eye and said, "You'd better be thinking about the hereafter." Burl's uncle sent Granny B money regularly for many years because he knew she would have a hard time raising her young children. Times were hard enough back then; especially for a young widow. She had a son named Connie, whose nickname was "Ji." And I don't know how to spell it. Or why. "Whee, why just why that's why."

His wife, Anner, died young and left him with two children to raise. A boy and a girl. As so often happened in those days, Connie and his children moved in with his mother. His daughter's name was Lillian, but even girl's had nicknames - hers was Widd. His son was Robert Angle and was "afflicted." The word retarded was not known in Pollard. Such people were either feeble minded, afflicted, not right or half a bubble off plumb. There were no special education classes, no special education schools, usually people like that were sent to the feeble minded institution. But Bob Angle stayed with Granny B until she died. Occasionally two or three young boys would see him out of

Granny B's sight and tease him. He simply did not know how to react to this and would hold his arms up in the air and say, "Ahh, goo." He was a gentle soul and went to church every time the doors were opened and always sat on the front row. He also went to the altar every night during each revival. And every Sunday, in the summer time, he followed Esther's Aunt Banty or some other family home from church for Sunday dinner. Everyone was kind to him and would seat him at the table with them to eat. After a big fried chicken dinner and all the trimmings, Bob Angle would get up from the table and say, "Well, how much do I owe you?" And of course, the answer was always "Nary a thing." Until one Sunday the head of the household decided to play a little trick. "Oh, that'll be about a dollar" Bob Angle was so taken aback he just stood there and finally he remembered something Granny B had told him that would be applicable in this situation. He turned to his host and said. "Be sure your sins will find you out." And I wonder how many times Mommy Johns has said that very same thing to Esther and me! When Granny B died, Robert Angle spent his remaining years in the Feeble Minded Institute in Frankfort. Bobby Fain visited him a few years later and Bob Angle asked him to move in with him saying "We could have lots of fun." And with Bobby he would have had lots of fun.

Vic had his first experience with home brew near a pond below Granny B's house. It was quite common for the man of the house to have a secret hiding place where he made a bit of home brew or even moonshine likker. One summer night Vic was on his way to the store, when he heard Connie whistling. He walked over, found Connie bottling a fresh batch of homebrew, and being the neighborly sort, offered his services. Connie had a scrunched up tin can, which he used as a funnel. Vic sampled any amount remaining in the can. Or perhaps one bottle was a bit too full. Anyway, when the job was finished, Vic reached over to grab a cornstalk for a little help in getting to his feet. Well, the cornstalk wasn't where he thought it was and he fell in the pond. Connie pulled him out and he went on out to the store.

In the hills of Pollard, there was no such thing as social drinking. A man could go along for weeks, months, occasionally even a year and never touch a drop. But just let someone say "There's a new batch been run off down below the Bill Ev hillside" and they were drinkin, layin out and gamblin and worrying their poor wives and mothers half to death.

Now, let there be no mistake, the head of the household was always the husband. He made all financial decisions, ruled the roost entirely, EXCEPT where alcohol was concerned. And that's when the wife stepped in. No whiskey, no homebrew, no wine, no moonshine was allowed her house. So, all imbibing was done in someone's barn, corncrib or quite often in some holler. And they drank to get drunk and stayed drunk for anywhere from three days to three weeks. Now, I'm not talking about everyone, just the ones who had not been saved.

Another couple that lived in Pollard was Ocie and Bob Butler. Ocie was said to have had very loose morals when she was very young and was caught giving one of the uncles a bath. And I would have to be drawn and quartered before I tell which one that was. I just happened to think: it should have been Uncle Clay.

They had no children, but considered themselves to be parents of a little white fluffy lap dog, named Trixie. Everyone owned dogs and cats, but their lineage was always suspect and the word pedigree might as well been of foreign derivation. (If I tried to sneak a kitten or puppy in the house, it was always "Get that nasty thing out of here.") Trixie was allowed the run of the house and was as pampered and petted as any child. This so disgusted one of the locals, that he was heard to remark, "If you'd stick a broomstick up its hind-end, it 'ud make a real good dust mop." When Trixie died, Ocie purchased a child-sized coffin from Betts and Smithers funeral home and buried her in one corner of the yard.

She was also the local contributor to the Jessamine Journal, a weekly newspaper that printed news from various communities, such as Little Hickman, Pollard, Kissing Ridge, and Antioch. If someone went to Nicholasville on Saturday, we read about it the following week. Once we read that Mr. and Mrs. Calvin Comley spent Sunday with Mr. and Mrs. Owen Comley. That was a big joke in Pollard because everyone knew that we spent every Sunday with them. A visit from such distinguished relatives as Uncle Henry and Aunt Sarah was really a news item.

Ocie loved children and Vic and I were her favorites. He was more favored than I was. She often cared for us and on one occasion took us to Lexington and had our photographs made. She and Bob left Pollard, moved to Lexington and lived there many years.

Ocie Butler, Alma Sebastian Johns and Esther Johns (baby) about 1928

We always had several cats for not only did Daddy like cats, they were needed to control the mouse population. We also had several dogs, but the one I remember most is a mutt named Ol' Carl. Dogs were, with the exception of Trixie, usually named good old dog names. There was always a Fido, Rover or Spot, Ring, etc.

Cats were so commonplace, that they didn't even have names. They were simply called, "Here, kitty," Animals were definitely not a part of the family as referred to in today's society. Pet food had yet to be invented, and if it had been, no one would have or could have bought it. They were fed left over scraps from the table and they supplemented that by catching an unsuspecting rabbit or squirrel. Occasionally, some farm dog would learn how to rob a hen's nest and suck out the contents of the egg necessitating the disposal of the dog. This is the origin of the saying "There's nothing more low down than a suck egg dog."

Great Uncle Lark Fain bought the first car in Pollard - a 1926 Model T Ford. He never learned to drive it, so Dad simply took possession of it, driving it to Nicholasville and Lexington several times a week. It was always a source of worry and annoyance to Grandad that Daddy never had any interest in farming and one day someone asked him if Dad was out plowing for the spring crops, Grandad said, "No, that plow's got no windshield." Every year, on the first glorious spring day, Dad would go outside, stand around for a few minutes, then come back in and say, "This weather makes me want to get out and grub." Mother simply looked at him and with a sniff and a small grin and returned to whatever she was doing. He always (as we knew he would) managed to resist that impulse and was soon on his way to Lexington, Nicholasville, and the mountains or anywhere except a hillside that needed plowing or "grubbing."

One day, Uncle Ira decided he wanted to go to Lexington with dad. When they arrived in Lexington, Dad parked the car, got out and went about his business and left Uncle Ira to do his own thing. The story goes that he sat in the car all day, because he knew absolutely nothing about how to get around Lexington.

Later Dad bought a truck and after one of those all day trips, we never knew what would be loaded on the truck, for everywhere he went, he talked someone into selling him something that he could resell. And if he couldn't sell it immediately, not to worry, he'd store it in the barn and some day someone would come along and need just that very thing. Speaking of barns, one of my favorite pastimes was prowling around in a barn. I had access to three barns and remember every hayloft, stall, corncrib and stripping room (For all my city born and bred children and grandchildren, that was not a room in the barn where we disrobed, that was where tobacco was stripped and tied into hands) in all of them. Barns were so cool in the summer time, and cold in the wintertime, with the exception of the stripping room where a small heater helped, but not very much. I wandered off again there, didn't I?

I can't write about Pollard and leave out Harrison and Ann Hurt. Harrison grew up in Kissing Ridge and Ann grew up in Scufflesville (also known as One Cup.) They were the parents of seven children of their own and although they lived in a four room house located in a holler about halfway between Uncle Larkin's store and Garland's store, they "took in" anyone else who needed a place to stay or even a place to live. Everyone was welcome. Houston Brumfield was practically a full time resident as was his sister, Reba. Their upstairs bedroom was always full and running over with kinfolks or not kinfolks. Made no difference. They welcomed everyone. Ann's older brother lost his eyesight and had no one else to care for him, so she and Harrison welcomed him into their home, and she cared for him until he died. Aunt Minnie said that if she were without a home, she'd go to Harrison's and Ann's, as they would take in anybody. If she had, she'd have had plenty to eat for Ann was known all over Pollard as being an outstanding cook. Her specialty was fried fish and Harrison's specialty was catching them. She cooked for neighbors when there was illness or a death and even washed and ironed clothes for "Aunt Janie" Peel when she was sick. The two daughters, Hazel and Marie rode a mule named Ol' Beck to deliver the clean clothes. They were a fun loving family.

They were always having fish fries and musical entertainment. Hazel played the guitar and when she married Malcolm Masters a party was enjoyed at the home place. Victor remembers hearing a mandolin for the first time and thought it the sweetest sound he'd ever heard. Marie and I went to school together and saw the same Saturday afternoon western movies when we were children. One serial starred an Indian girl named Nyoka. Marie liked the name so much that when she married Slick Moberly at the age of fourteen, she named their only daughter Nyoka. When Hazel died, a wealth of Pollard lore died with her. Even Vic has been known to call on her a time or two when he couldn't get someone's relatives straightened out. During the 1937 flood, Malcolm and Harrison took their boats and went to Louisville to help. When someone handed a small blanket wrapped bundle out a window to Mike, he handled it carefully. It turned out to be a cat.

Pollard housewives were just like their "town" sisters in one way. They all loved flowers. But front porch containers were of a different sort. If a granite pan no longer held water, it was filled with barnyard dirt and chicken manure and flowers grew like Jack's beanstalk. One Pollard housewife even made use of a discarded slop jar and she lived right on Pollard Road. But petunias cascading down the sides disguised the shape and added beauty to an otherwise unadorned door step. And worn out truck tires filled with marigolds graced many a front yard.

When Bill and I were newly married and living in Louisville on Gheens Avenue, one male resident fancied himself quite a gardener. Bill dug a little plot in front of the house and we made a weekend trip to Pollard. I came back with a big bag of chicken manure, mixed it in with that Louisville dirt and sowed several packages of zinnias and marigolds. As luck would have it, a light rain fell that night and about two days later tiny zinnia leaves were poking thought the dirt. J.C. had a hard time living with that, but he shouldn't have, because he was born in the eastern Kentucky Mountains, and I'm sure they had manure there, too.

Mommy Johns could stick any kind of plant in the ground and it wouldn't dare wilt.

Lest you all think that Pollard produced only farmers, a few carpenters, and gristmill operators that simply isn't true. Charlie Wylie was born on Kissin' Ridge, became an attorney and went on to serve in the state legislature. He always told everyone that he was from Pollard and the farther back one lived on Kissin' Ridge, the meaner one was, and bragged that he lived in the last house on the left. His brother, Burch Wylie became one of Nicholasville's most beloved dentists.

And then there was the most famous native of all - my big brother. Most of his career was spent as the Executive Secretary of the State Highway Contractors Association. In 1998 the Construction Management Founders Society honored him by giving him a Lifetime Achievement Award. I like to think that mother, daddy, Grandad and Granny knew about that. And I know that somehow Mother found a way to tell Aunt Minnie.

Sickness, Death and Funerals

These were the days before Medicare and nursing homes came into being and folks called a doctor only in dire emergencies. Some even lived their entire lives without ever having seen a doctor. A yearly check-up would have been ridiculed as utter foolishness, for unless the disease was obvious to the naked eye or could be heard through the doctor's stethoscope, he had no way of diagnosing the ailment. There were no cat-scans, no ultrasounds, or EKG's. All the patient could do was tell the doc where it hurt and hope for the best. Most women had their babies at home or, as did my mother, went to the home of her parents. Childbirth did sometimes require the ministrations of a physician, but few other ailments were thought to be serious enough to warrant the expense of Dr. Welch or Dr. Williams.

A liberal dousing of coal oil healed cuts and scratches. When Victor was about six, as he was cutting kindling, the hatchet slipped and he sliced his thumb to the bone. Mother replaced the flesh and skin, grabbed the only cloth available, a piece of tobacco canvas, and bandaged the wound. She then soaked thumb and bandage in coal oil and it healed completely without ever being sore. He does have a sizable scar to show for his carelessness.

When Pollard folks were sick, neighbors took food and went to set up, meaning to spend the night relieving exhausted family members. One neighbor would set up one night, another the next night, and occasionally, when death was imminent, there would be a room full. This was also a form of macabre entertainment, for there was no television and very few people had radios. So this was not only a chance to help a neighbor, it was a chance to visit and socialize. There were few automobiles and transportation to help the sick was mostly by horse and buggy, mule, or by walking.

Granny told the story of going to set up with a woman who lived down on the river. People who lived down on the river were below today's so called poverty level. We had little in the way of material things, but wealth has always been a matter of comparison, and these people were so abjectly poor, that in comparison to them, we lived like Rockefellers. Wellll, not really. We called them River Rats. Nevertheless, they were people in need, so Granny baked one of her best transparent pies and went to see if she could be of some assistance.

She arrived around suppertime and after seeing that the family was fed and the dishes washed, as was the custom, took her bedside vigil beside the patient. This small shanty had no screen door and the front door was left open for any cooling breeze. Around dusk, came the laying hens, first one, and then another, followed by a third until the whole flock had come in to roost upon the foot of the iron bed. As chickens will do, they tucked their heads under a wing and dozed off into chicken dreamland. The man of the house soon came in and turned all the chickens around until their behinds faced the door. This was done to avoid any nighttime mess on the bed.

Most old people died at home or, in some instances, in the home of a daughter or son. If they had neither kinfolks nor money, they were forced to go to the Poor House, where they relied on the county to provide care in their last days. Occasionally, older relatives had financially strapped grandchildren to move in with them. This was the case with Great Grandpa Milford. His brother, Larkin, had married a beautiful young woman from Madison County She died at a very young age and Uncle Lark never remarried, so Grandpa Milford went to live with his brother. Then Uncle Lark preceded him in death and Grandpa Milford had become feeble and it became Mothers lot to care for him. We were living in that little house that was owned by Rhody Miller, and I was about four years old. So our family moved to Grandpa Milford's house just below the store. I remember very little about his personality, but it's strange how I can recall every feature of his face and can't do the same with some of the other long dead relatives. He had a full mustache, a receding hairline and age splotches all over his face. At mealtime, he always asked for a refill on buttermilk, and when the glass was about two thirds full, he'd say, "Tha." That was his way of saying, "There, that's all I want." I suppose that was how he was immortalized. For years, when iced tea, milk or water was served, someone would say, "Tha" and we all thought of Grandpa Milford.

Granny was behind the door when the Good Lord passed around patience.

Uncle Lark probably had hardening of the arteries, for he often didn't know what was going on and imagined he saw things that no one else could see. Once he thought he saw birds on the ceiling, and no one could convince him otherwise. She kept telling him there were no birds there and finally picked up a broom, swept the ceiling, and said, "Now, hush, about birds on the ceiling." Mother would never have said anything like that; she was always so kind to old people.

Grandpa Milford was the great-great-great grandson of William Fain, who died about 1839. His first wife was Elizabeth Stinnett. They had two children, Ida and Ludora. Aunt Idy lived to be in her nineties and it was a local legend that during her lifetime she never washed her hair. She simply combed it with a very fine-toothed comb. That was the same style of comb that was used to get rid of lice and their eggs. If Granny was behind the door when patience was passed out, than Aunt Idy was behind the door when tact was passed out. And I was under the house when both were passed out. Aunt Idy had been invited to a big country dinner, and after viewing all the food, said, "Well, you've got enough clabber cheese to feed your chickens for a week." Clabber cheese was what we know as cottage cheese and was usually fed to the chickens, but this hostess obviously thought her clabber cheese was good enough to serve to "company."

After Elizabeth died, Milford married Bette Davis, a widow from Madison County. She had two children by her first husband, Aunt Dona Masters and Aunt Claudia English. Together, they had three children, Uncle Larkin, Uncle Ira, and Laura, who was our Granny.

When Granny Bett died, Milford moved in with his brother, Larkin, and they lived together until Larkin's death. Mother cared for him for about four years.

I remember being sent to get Uncle Ira the evening he was dying. I was also told to remain there until sent for.

This was in 1935 and no one ever thought of taking the deceased to a funeral home. Funeral homes, at that time, were not the sophisticated establishments that they are today. They embalmed the body, transported it to a church, then to a graveyard and completed the rite by actual interment. When Grandpa Milford died, the undertaker was called to his house and from there he transported the body to Granny's house where he performed the embalming procedure. Bill Betts, of Betts and Smithers asked Victor, who was about fourteen, if he would like to watch. And he did.

After the body was washed, it was dressed in a suit that he'd probably had for fifty years and placed in a casket. It was then taken to the front room, lifted upon a stretcher, where it remained for two days. In its immobile state for all to gaze upon. And wonder. And listen. "Don't he look natural?" "Just like he was sleeping." He didn't. He looked pale, waxen, artificial and dead dead dead.

A black funeral wreath was hung on the front door. Its purpose was not decorative, but was hung there to signify that death had made its unwelcome presence in that household. These wreaths were the property of the funeral establishments and were usually made of black satin that had been folded and sewn to resemble a rose. If someone had been ill for a few weeks or months and upon passing by, we saw that black wreath, we knew that another soul had gone to the great beyond.

To a nine-year-old child, there was nothing so mysterious as death. Especially if that nine year old child was a product of a family that never discussed or explained. If we asked questions, and wondered why, the standard answer was, "whee, why, just why, that's why." We formed our own opinions, and somehow, we survived.

Via the country grapevine, word was spread that there was a death in the community. The neighbors and relatives started bringing food, with each housewife trying to outdo the other. Every cook put forth her best effort when her particular specialty was on display for all to see. Fried chicken was usually the first to appear on the table, and then followed dressed eggs by the dozen. And cakes and pies, cobblers vied for space on the kitchen table.

Weather permitting, the men usually stood outside, leaning against tree trunks, smoking roll your own cigarettes, and sometimes having a little nip while women busied themselves in the kitchen, serving food, washing dishes, and dispensing emotional support.

After outside chores were attended to, for cows had to be fed and milked come hell or high water, dishes were washed, food was put away and everyone visited and mourned for a while. All but two or three men returned to their own homes, but someone remained to sit up with the body. They stayed awake throughout the night sitting there by lamplight. They usually sat up two nights, for to have buried someone the next day would have shown a lack of respect for the deceased and would have been the subject of much scandalized discussion.

When all the near and far relatives had made their way back to the home place, the body was taken to Mt. Beulah church, where it was placed in front of the altar. Sprays of flowers were placed to each side of the casket. The number of floral offerings depended upon the wealth of the deceased and the survivors. So did the quality of the casket. Everyone wanted to put away their loved ones in high style so they wouldn't be talked about and said to be uncaring. Of course, they were talked about either way, "They sure did put him away good, what do you reckon that casket cost?" Or the opposite, "Did you notice that pine box they laid him out in?"

The casket was always open for viewing during the service; no one could see him with the exception of the front row occupants.

Brother Willie Peel was one of our area's most famous preachers. Methodist preacher's names were always preceded by the title, Brother, and Brother Willie Peel was seldom referred to as Brother Peel or Brother Willie. He was always Brother Willie Peel. His main claim to fame was that he never preached less than a three handkerchief funeral; meaning that mourners should come prepared with at least three clean handkerchiefs. He usually had the tears started with the opening prayer.

If the deceased were female, he'd start with, "Oh, I've eaten many a biscuit at this dear lady's table." The good Lord knows that was the truth, for Methodist preachers were noted for their ability to dispose of everything on the table. He would then start talking about the poor motherless children and the loving husband who was now without his life's partner. This was good for at least one handkerchief. Then we would all hear of the good Christian lady and her dedication to her church, and, "Oh, how we'll all miss her." Everyone started on the second handkerchief. As if that were not enough, there were all the old Methodist Hymns, "Precious Memories", "Shall we Gather at the River?", "Will the Circle be Unbroken" and "In the Sweet By and By." All beloved old songs; all capable of making the heart and soul weep. During the second verse of "In the Sweet By and By" the third handkerchief was soggy and it was time for Bill Betts to come from the rear of the church to direct the mourners past the open casket for one last good bye. Bill Betts was another one of those characters that were seldom referred to by a shortened version of his name.

Bill Betts' walk from the rear of the church to the casket was different from his normal every day stride. When the last stanza had been sung, the last "Amen" uttered, Brother Willie Peel said, "The undertaker will now take charge." Bill Betts straightened his spine, stuck his belly out a bit more than usual, hitched up his pants, and with a sorrowful respectful expression, swaggered to the front of the church. Vic can do an imitation of Bill Betts that is better than Bill Betts himself.

Each row of mourners, starting at the back of the church was called to the front for a last viewing and gently nudged past the casket by Bill Betts. Occasionally, a bit of prodding was needed when a brokenhearted relative or friend was reluctant to move on. Ocie Butler could never pass an open casket without pausing, reaching in and touching the deceased on the forehead.

Then the front row occupants were led for a final viewing. They were the relatives who had to say one last goodbye. Bill Betts closed the casket lid forever more and it was loaded into the gaping rear end of the hearse to be carried to its final resting place. This vehicle was always driven by Bill Betts and was followed by mourners in order of their relationship to the deceased. If the funeral procession met another vehicle going in the opposite direction, the driver of the car, truck or horse and buggy always pulled over to the side of the road and came to a complete stop. This signified respect for the dead. That didn't happen too often, which was just as well, for those roads were very narrow. Horses were always wary of cars and required a steady hand to keep them calm.

Grandpa Milford was laid to rest in the Fain graveyard. After the funeral procession arrived at the cemetery, final prayers were said, another hymn was sung then close friends and relatives returned to the home of the deceased. Food was served from the mountainous supply brought in by friends and neighbors. They sat around the kitchen table, out on the front porch, in the front room and told stories about the dear departed. These were always funny stories or loving stories and by bedtime, the deceased had been elevated to a much higher position than he or she had ever dreamed of reaching in real life.

Occasionally, following a funeral, someone would go out to Garland's store and conversation would be something like this. Listen:

Hidy, where ye been?

Hidy. been to Ol' Man Milford's funeral.

Was there a lot of people there?

Yeah, a right smart crowd.

Did the family take it hard?

Well, yeah, and a'course Ocie had to stop at the casket and pat him on the face and stand there and look at him a long time.

Then followed a long discussion of the emotional reaction of all the survivors, who cried most, who cried least. Funerals were, in a way, another form of entertainment.

People in Pollard were most always buried in family graveyards, and since so many people were directly or indirectly related to each other, there were usually plots available in one graveyard or another.

The Comleys have a graveyard on River Road but since Comleys no longer live in Pollard, it is over grown with weeds and brush, some of the tombstones are broken and moss covered and the area is enclosed with a double strand of barbed wire attached to sadly leaning fence posts. There lies Great-Grandpa Jerry, Grandad's father. Jerry was first married to Marthy Jane Murphy, who had an unmarried sister named Susan. It was not uncommon in that era, for two or three families to live in one house. In this instance, Susan made her home with Marthy Jane and Jerry.

Now what was uncommon (actually, that was very common of him!) was that while he was having a family with Marthy Jane, he was also having a second family with Susan. In fact, one of Marthy Jane's children and one of Susan's were only three months apart in age. Jerry and Marthy Jane had eight children and when she died at the age of forty-three, he married Susan and they had one more child (after the two born out of wedlock.) Grandad was a product of the union of Jerry and Marthy Jane. I knew nothing of all this when I was growing up, but I knew that Grandad had a half-brother and some half-sisters.

They were our great-aunts and great-uncles and we visited them, they visited us, just one big family. I vaguely remember some reference to Jerry climbing in and out of Susan's window while he was married to Marthy Jane but since children were to be seen and not heard, I was probably sent to go draw a fresh bucket of water or something.

Some of the sisters in that family had what Victor calls the Murphy curse. (Great Grandpa Jerry married a Murphy.) As they became older, their voices developed a strong quiver reminiscent of the way Katharine Hepburn now sounds. When Vic developed an interest in genealogy, he called on Aunt Margaret House, and asked her about the three months age difference between those two babies. She was slightly embarrassed, as she looked at him, and with a shaky trembling voice, said *"Aw, you know the story."* and that's all she would say about it. Several children of these two unions are buried in the Comley graveyard. Speaking of Vic's interest in genealogy, he searched back as far as one Erasmus Comley, and decided that he'd gone far enough. I've always thought that such a funny story and have told it several times. Once, when I told it to my Danish friend, Annie Edwards, she informed me that Erasmus was a fine old Danish name, and the story lost its punch line. I really drifted there, well, back to graveyards.

The Fain Graveyard is located in Pollard, near where Uncle Ira and Aunt Annie lived; in fact it is almost in the front yard. It is there that Granny and Grandad were laid to rest. The House graveyard is located between Pollard and Uncle Larkin's store. Legend has it that after one of the Stinnetts was buried there; some of the House clan seemed to think that a Stinnett was unworthy of spending eternity with the Houses. The Stinnett survivors, being a proud lot, were so insulted that they had the body dug up and started their own graveyard.

Down near the river is a small community called Antioch. There is a still active church, and a nearby graveyard. Dru Reynolds was a resident of Antioch, and as in some small communities, there is always one person whom small boys enjoy pestering. Dru might be out in her yard, minding her own business, when three or four boys walked by, and said, "Psst, Dru!" For some unknown reason, that made her furious. She always threw rocks at them, while they ran away, saying "Psst, Dru!" until out of sight. She also said if she lived and nothing happened, she wanted to be buried at Antioch.

Then there is the Reynolds graveyard on Kissin Ridge. Vic and I drove out that road recently and it is one of the best kept country graveyards I have ever seen. I asked Bob Fain if he knew the difference between a graveyard and a cemetery. He said in cemeteries, graves were always dug by machinery and in graveyards, graves were always dug by someone like Big Ern.

Farm families always came from far and wide to pull weeds, paint fences and plant flowers on Decoration Day. The relative who lived closest to the graveyard usually hosted the dinner, which was brought by everyone. The Peel family alone could get everything finished in time for a back to the house visit and cake and ice cream. Aunt Lizzie and Uncle Willie had fourteen children. Mother and Daddy are buried in Nicholasville where perpetual care is available.

Great Great Uncle Larkin Fain's wife, Amelia Masters Fain

Amusements and Entertainment

With the exception of a few toys left by Santy Claus every year there were very few bought toys in our family. Or any other family. I probably had more than most Pollard children, for when I was six or seven Mother and Daddy lived in Lexington during the winter and worked for Reynolds Tobacco Company. They always came home on weekends and stocked up on food for the following week.

I can remember only two Christmases. In reality, I think I remember only one. The first one was one of those supposedly cute child stories that was told so many times that I merely imagine I remember it. When I was about three years old, we were living in a two-room house owned by Monroe Miller. Practically next to the Reynolds graveyard. If I had been old enough, I would have been frightened of ghosts. Anyway, I slept with Mother and Daddy and Victor stayed with Granny and Grandad.

We never had a Christmas tree in all the years that I lived in Pollard. My folks would have thought such carryins on to be foolish. And Daddy was apt to celebrate Christmas the same way that so many of the uncles did so the adults were seldom in a festive state of mind.

One reads so much about fruit cakes being baked right after Thanksgiving, and left to season. Granny could have made hers the day before Christmas and it would have been pronounced delicious. She didn't bake her cake as did most people. Hers was steamed in a huge roasting pan somewhat in the way of an English Plum Pudding. They really didn't need seasoning for they were moist and could have been sliced as soon as they had set.

But on that Christmas morning, in 1929, I awoke and ran to the corner where Santa had left a pile of toys. Wonder of Wonders! I picked up the most outstanding of all and ran back to my parent's bed and said, "Look! Look! Look at my little pea organ!" Santa had left a few other things but nothing created the wide-eyed wonder as that little miniature piano.

I actually remember the Christmas of my sixth year. We were all spending the night at Grannies and Grandad's house, because Mother and Daddy always rented a small apartment in Lexington and worked at the re-dryer. They had come home for the weekend and on Christmas morning; there in the corner was a beautiful baby doll. I had to run upstairs to show this prize to Mother and Daddy after their less than enthusiastic admiration, I ran back downstairs to see what else Santa had left. Other than the actual acquisition, dolls were not all that exciting for me.

We never knew when, but sometime during the Christmas season, Dad brought home a big sack of candy, fruit and nuts. Brazil nuts, English walnuts, Hazelnuts, pecans.

We only had these at Christmas and it was a source of pride for me to take two English walnuts in my hands and squeeze them together until one or both cracked. Often I could pick the thin shells away until the walnut remained in one piece.

There was always a big peppermint stick for Grandad as this was his favorite candy. They resembled a miniature barber pole. Other Christmas candies had a design in the center, such as a rose or a Christmas tree, and that remained identifiable as long as a sliver remained. The pink cushion shaped candies had soft centers with an unfamiliar taste. They were not very good but we sampled each one. I had never tasted perfume or talcum powder but that's what they smelled like. My favorite of the hard candies was the red cinnamon flavored ribbons. We also had lots of oranges. They were as much fun to play with as they were to eat. After the orange was eaten, Vic or I would crease the peeling and one of us would sneak up behind the other and squeeze the peel in an eye. This produced a reddened, stinging eye that could only be relieved by revenge. It was also great fun to squeeze the creased peeling over a lighted match and see the resulting blue, red and orange flames. "You two will wet the bed if you don't stop playing with fire!"

When Esther and I were very small, we had what we called Play Houses. We sat under a big maple tree in Mommy's front yard and from a tin bucket or granite pan we removed our collection of rocks, sticks, and pieces of broken glass and pottery. These we arranged to form a semblance of a house. Room by room. Grown-ups called these our play pretties. "Go get your play-pretties and don't bother us while we're canning, I'll declare to my time it don't seem like a body can ever get caught up with all the work there is to do around here." This was before Daddy brought home the really and truly doll furniture and Mommy Johns gave us the use of that out building across from the one time carriage house.

Cooking and playing house in that one-time corncrib was probably our favorite activity, but making mud pies out on Johns Lane ran a close second. We had our favorite spot, which was about fifty yards past Mommy's red barn. After finding our stirring spoons, and drawing a bucket of water from the well, we started walking to our spot. Nowhere else did the sun shine so brightly in a sky so blue. Nowhere else were the few clouds such a pearly white. And nowhere else were two little girls so happily anticipating a fun filled day. A side trip through the barn was an added enticement. Perhaps we might see a new calf or find a hidden nest of chickens or guineas. If not, maybe we should climb up in the barn loft to see what's there. (The same thing that was up there yesterday, last week, and year before last, for no farm family ever threw anything away!) Instead of climbing down the same way we climbed up, we jumped down. That was fun, let's do that again. Then on to our spot, which had the softest, fluffiest, rock free dirt of any road in Jessamine County. Since we were bare footed, we made footprints in the dirt, watched it puff up between our toes and then sat down to make the nicest mud pies in Pollard. We expertly mixed the correct amount of water and dirt, stirred until it reached the perfect consistency, then patted out pies by the dozens. This was a wonderful substitute for Play Dough. They were left in the hot sun to harden and were abandoned until another day. We brushed off our dresses, bloomers and legs and went back to the house but not until we made a quick trip down to the garden where we found summer-ripened tomatoes and had a quick snack - dust and all.

Girls played jacks by the hour. No one could ever be sure which way the ball would bounce on those uneven linoleum covered floors, but that was just part of the game. We still played onezies and twozies, touch-me-nots and bird in a cage.

We climbed trees; I still have a light scar as a result of falling from a big maple in Mommy's yard. We explored under her house, we waded the small streams between "them hollers" and climbed up and down slick waterfalls. We found black raspberry vines and ate until we were stuffed. We made clover chains and wore them around our necks, pretending them real necklaces. When we tired of that, we found honeysuckle vines, pulled blossoms and sucked the sweetness from the bottom. For another taste sensation, we pulled sourgrass to chew and pucker our mouths.

Sears Roebuck Catalog had uses besides a substitute for toilet tissue and rolling pretend cigarettes. We sat on the floor and cut out marvelous paper doll families. There were pretty mothers with finger waved hair, handsome rugged fathers and sturdy, healthy, well-dressed children. The flip of a page and a snip of the scissors could change their clothes. We called these catalogs wish books. We wished we owned everything pictured on every page.

We roamed all over Pollard, weirdo child molesters were unheard of and we were completely unsupervised. I might leave the house some morning, my destination being Mommy Johns' house, change my mind half way there and go to see Aunt Dallas. She owned a player piano (the only one in Pollard) and she always let us insert a roll of music. All we had to contribute was foot power by pressing the foot pedals.

Boys and girls were more or less segregated. Boys had their space and girls had theirs. Boys played marbles; country children called them marvels, and occasionally shot at birds with slingshots, until the offending weapon was confiscated by Miss Gin and kept in her desk drawer until school ended for the summer. No matter, any self respecting country boy could make a new one in "two shakes of a lamb's tail." (That's faster than a New York minute.) The fork of a strong hard wood tree was cut, leaving about four inches below the fork to be used as a stock. Two strips of rubber from a discarded inner tube and a piece of leather completed the makings of a slingshot. One end of each of the rubber strips was fastened to each side of the fork and the other to the leather pouch. Place a small rock in the leather pouch, hold the stock firmly in one hand with the leather piece holding the stone between the thumb and forefinger of the other hand, pull back and let 'er rip. A slingshot can be a fairly dangerous contraption.

We caught June bugs and tied a long piece of thread around a hind leg just to see how long we could keep one flying. A June bug is an iridescent hard-shelled beetle that is about an inch long, The flying, angry bug was similar to flying a kite, and we didn't have to wait until March winds. On hot summer nights, we chased the "Now you see them, now you don't" fireflies or lightening bugs as we called them. They were somewhat frustrating, for just when we thought we'd caught one, he'd turn off his little flashlight and reappear two or three yards from where he should have been.

Victor fashioned yo-yos from wooden spools and made peashooters from elder bushes. The elder bush limbs had white pithy centers which, when reamed out, made very satisfactory weapons.

A discarded automobile tire furnished hours of amusement for daredevil boys. One boy curled up inside, had a buddy stand the tire upright and at the proper moment, gave tire and boy a shove down one of those hill sides. I never tried that, I didn't trust the tire to absorb all that shock if I ran into something.

I read everything I had access to. Which wasn't very much. Pollard School didn't have a library so most of my reading material came from boxes of junk, partial estates, etc., that Daddy brought home. He also liked to read True Story magazines and True Confessions and brought home a new issue every month. Mother never read such trash and didn't want me to either, but I always did. My reading material certainly was a contrast. One day I read True Story or True Confession, the next day I read one of The Elsie Dinsmore books. This kept me in an emotional and conscientious turmoil. Elsie Dinsmore was a pious little goody-goody who almost thought breathing was a sin. Especially if she breathed on Sunday. She loved her father better than anyone on this earth, but he was not at all religious, and had no patience with her fanaticism. They had a continuing battle about her piano playing. She thought it a sin to play the piano on Sunday, and that's the only time he seemed to want her to play. But come hell or high water, she wouldn't play a note on Sunday. She was heartbroken because she had disobeyed her beloved father, I believe she called him "Papa" though. Anyway, one day I'm saying "Poor Elsie", and worrying about my going to hell, and considering letting "Aunt" Laurey Locker talk me into going down to that alter during next summer's revival. The next day I'm hiding in a closet, reading True Story and trying to imagine what happened when that good looking man took that beautiful woman in his arms and it said, "Continued next month." FOR SURE--they didn't spell it out for you back then! Lord, I wished I had someone to talk to.

I don't remember the word vacation being in our vocabulary. Oh, someone might take a trip to Ohio, to see an aunt or uncle, but the idea of going to Florida or somewhere like that was unheard of. For one thing, it was hot enough in Pollard and there was entirely too much work to be done, and if there was any extra money, it was kept in the bank, because hard times might be just around the corner.

Earning Money

Children of my generation had no concept of the word "allowance." The idea of paying a child for household work was absolutely unheard of. People had large families for two reasons. Number one, there was no sure means of birth control, and number two, large families were needed to help with all the farm work.

Eggs were used as a monetary unit, and we were fortunate to wheedle one to take to the store and exchange it for a piece of candy or gum. Granny was a soft touch and would always spring for one or two to be carried to the store in a hot little hand. One egg could be exchanged for two cents worth of candy. Never in my entire childhood did I ever drop one. Farm wives hoarded hen eggs to be taken to the store and sold or traded for fabric, sugar, shoes or anything not grown on the farm.

There were few ways for a young girl to earn money. Since mothers were the primary source of food for babies, where the mother went, the baby went. So baby sitters were a thing of the future. Older children were left at home when the mother was called upon to attend to some neighbor in need or to help with the farm work. There was usually a resident grandmother or old maid aunt who fulfilled the role of a baby sitter and they didn't charge a fee. If the mother happened to be unavoidably detained, and it was past the baby's feeding time a sugar tit made a passable if not nutritional substitute. A spoon full of sugar was placed on a clean white cloth, approximately four inches square, and was molded into the shape of a nipple then stuck into the baby's mouth until the real thing arrived.

One summer, I picked about twelve gallons of blackberries and earned enough money to pay for my first "permanent wave." I had a head full of frizz that didn't look at all like the pictures in True Story magazine.

For weeks I had envisioned myself as one of those lovely models. I was so disappointed when I saw in the mirror that it was the same old freckled faced me. With the exception of frizzy hair.

There were a few other means of earning money. I remember working in the tobacco patches. I know of no other job that is as demanding, dirty or as hard on the back. Even a twelve or thirteen year old back aches when one has dropped or set tobacco plants all day. The first time I ever worked in tobacco, it was set by hand. A hole was dug in the plowed row with a tobacco peg, and then someone dropped the plant and mounded the soil around it. A few years later a much more sophisticated means of setting plants was available, when a tobacco setting apparatus was invented. This was no job for a girl. It required a man, preferably a strong man. This contraption consisted of a water tank, and a place for the plant to be dropped. At the top was a handle on either side. It was held and operated by one man, while someone else carried an armload of plants and dropped one in the setter. At the bottom were two sharp blades that fit together until inserted in the ground. Then in a quick sideways motion, dug a hole, released the plant and water simultaneously. How's that for modern technology?

Tobacco also requires hoeing, suckering, topping and worming. Suckering is removing new growth after it's already leafed out; topping has to be done when the plant is about three feet tall. The very top growth is broken off and discarded, discouraging tall lanky plants and resulting in a broader leaf. Worming is self-explanatory. When the plant was about two or three feet tall, they were usually attacked by ugly green hornworms. The green color was a result of their consumption of the tender green tobacco leaves. They had to be picked off by hand, pulled apart and dropped in a lard bucket. Using tobacco products was definitely harmful to their health! I don't remember how much I earned for worming tobacco, but whatever it was, it wasn't nearly enough.

One summer, one of our city cousins, Bill Henry Comley, spent a few weeks with us during tobacco season. When in Rome, do as the Romans do, so Bill Henry had to worm tobacco. Since he was a very fastidious person, that was not at all to his liking. He couldn't bring himself to pick them off by hand, so he placed a small stick in each hand and plucked them off without having to touch them. There's more than one way to skin a cat, or to kill a tobacco worm.

Tobacco plants exuded a substance that clung to the worker like a second skin. This was aptly called tobacco gum. It was sticky, gummy and was almost impossible to remove, even lye soap was ineffective. Of course, our lack of bathroom facilities was a hindrance also. We had to heat water on the stove, pour it into a granite pan about the size of a bathroom sink and that's the way we bathed. During tobacco season, we used a brand of soap called Lava Soap. It contained fine granular particles, and occasionally a bit of skin might be scrubbed off with the tobacco gum.

For a day's work in the tobacco fields, I was paid about four dollars. That was "good money" for the late thirties, and I felt quite affluent on our Saturday trips to Nicholasville. I was able to pay for my own movies and afterwards, always splurged on a "bought" hamburger from The Nicholasville Drug Store. A strawberry ice cream cone from Ward's Bakery usually topped this off. I know that sounds peculiar, buying an ice cream cone from a bakery, but Wards sold ice cream and baked goods.

Granny and Grandad's House

I have more memories of that house than any other house of my childhood. A rather simple structure, it was white and required paint rather than whitewash. Its only trim was a bit of decorative gingerbread at the top of either side of the porch posts. A tin roof covered it and everything that has been said about falling rain on a tin roof is absolute truth.

The Old Home Place - First House on Kissin' Ridge

The front porch stretched across the entire width of the house and provided an inviting place to relax when passersby stopped for a chat or a cool drink of water. A screeching, shrieking swing hung from the porch ceiling, and every time I swung too high I imagined those screws coming loose and sending the swing and me crashing to the floor. (The sky is falling.) It never did. The floor was painted gray and there were various lawn chairs and an occasional straight-backed kitchen chair brought out for Sunday afternoon company. Some of these kitchen chairs were so old and had been tilted so much that the back legs were an inch shorter than the front. Years later a small picket type two foot tall fence was added to the porch to keep the chickens from messing on the porch floor. It wasn't very effective for they were capable of flying a short distance. One summer Bill and I happened to be visiting with our two-year-old son, and an old rooster had perched upon the fence. When we opened the screen door, the rooster squawked, jumped a few inches in the air, flapped his wings and decided to leave before someone chased him off with a with a broom. Little Bill, who at that time was called Chip, had never seen a rooster. He stood there, awestruck, and then announced, "He did fan!"

I can close my eyes and see the slightly bulging wallpaper and the dark brown woodwork which I had helped Grandad paint. I can hear the faint squeak of the screen door opening into the sitting room. A giant maple tree shaded the house and on a hot summer day, to walk into that room was akin to walking into the air conditioning of today. Upon entering the room, the most outstanding piece of furniture was their blue and brass four-poster bed. Always with an immaculate white bedspread that didn't know the meaning of the word "wrinkle." Not everyone could make up a wrinkle free feather bed, but it really wasn't all that difficult. All one had to do was pick up each corner and shake all the feathers toward the middle. Then reach over and spread the feathers again to the corners, smoothing as they were patted and coaxed into their respective places. Each bed had its own "bolster," which was a long narrow pillow as wide as the bed. Nowadays, we all have our favorite soft downy pillow which, with a few thumps and punches, willingly conforms to a comfortable wad for sleeping. Well, let me tell you those bolsters were a piece of work. They conformed to no one! As a matter of fact, I always felt that it controlled me instead of my controlling it. Usually, upon awakening, that bolster was as dent free as it had been the night before. And try getting a clean starched bolster slip on one. If one is fortunate enough to still have only one chin, changing a pillowslip is a fairly easy task. Just put one end of the pillow between chin and neck, add a little pressure and use both hands to slide the clean slip over the pillow. When our children were small and we went to visit the farm, they enjoyed sleeping in the feather beds. Robin had to sleep with Bill, and she placed the bolster down the middle and neither could cross over to the other side.

A shiny linoleum "carpet" covered the floor and crisp lace curtains hung from the window. Grandad's big rocking chair was another familiar piece of furniture that always remained in the same place- directly in front of the fireplace. On the mantel, rested the fake marble Seth Thomas clock that announced its presence on the half-hour with a pleasant little "ting" and a more resounding "ching" on the hour, while striking the appropriate number. (Carol Ann has that clock now, but I don't think it pings or chings either one.) There was a miniature brown pottery teakettle which Vic now has on his mantel. Wonder which one of his children has "called" that? On one end of the mantel Daddy could always find his Jews Harp. When he was in a good mood, he liked to press that instrument to his front teeth, hold it with his left hand and twang out a tune or two by flipping the extended bar with his right middle finger. He would also sing a few verses of "Ramona" and "Molly and me, and Baby Makes Three." (I don't know why he ever thought that he could sing. He couldn't.) He also admitted to me that he couldn't dance either, but he could hold a woman while she danced.

To the right of the fireplace stood the dresser which held the kerosene lamp by which Victor studied and practiced spelling words. I'll be the first to admit that I didn't do much studying by any kind of light. Grandad sat in his rocking chair and "gave out" words for Victor to spell. "Spell "righid." He meant rigid. Spell "fer-tile." There were many other such mangled pronunciations, but something clicked, for Vic entered the regional spelling championship in the sixth grade, but didn't win. He was again Jessamine County's representative when he was in the eighth grade and this time, brought home the honors. He said that was the most significant thing he had accomplished. The story ran in the Lexington Herald Leader with a picture no less.

Grandad

The front room and the kitchen were made of logs and if a particularly wild spring storm was in progress, Mother and I always stayed in the front room until it passed on through. She told me that since that room was made of logs, it was a safe place to be and she was correct for it withstood many a storm (and several colonies of 'termanites.')

It was furnished with a wardrobe, which Grandad called a frigerolla, a chair or two, and a small table. Also in the front room was one of the world's first hide-a-beds. At that time they were called davenettes. They were as hard and uncomfortable as the proverbial brick. And ugly! The fabric was black and similar in texture to that from which buggy tops were made. Trim on the arms was oak. At nighttime it was unfolded to become my bed. That is, until I became old enough to sleep upstairs by myself. On the most frigid nights, I ran and jumped in bed, while Granny trailed along behind me, carrying a heavy quilt which she had heated by holding it in front of the fire. After wrapping that one around me, she then piled at least three more on top and I was on my own. There was a fire place in the room, but I can never remember it being used. On that mantel resided two chalk piano babies, one on either end. They stood guard over a milk glass shell upon which rested a porcelain Easter egg. This Victorian egg was an Easter present from Granny to Dad when he was a child of five. Victor has the surviving piano baby. One didn't make it through his four children. I have the saucer and egg.

The room adjacent to the kitchen was at one time the dining room, but I can't remember when it ceased being a dining room and became another bedroom. I do know that in the dead of winter, we raced through that room to get to the warmth of the kitchen. Providing someone had already built a fire in the big cook stove. And someone usually had.

When we went from room to room at night, we had to carry a lighted lamp with us, because there was no switch on the wall to flip and flood the room with light. Kitchen furniture consisted of the big farm table, covered with an oilcloth table cloth. Always on the table could be found the pressed glass spoon holder, a vinegar cruet (no one ate greens, wilted lettuce or souse without a big splash of vinegar.) Pinto beans are also very good with a jolt of vinegar. There were several different jars of jam or preserves and left over food to be eaten for supper. An immaculate white cloth covered all of this so no stray fly could light on the spoons or food. There was a pierced tin pie safe, a wash stand and granite wash pan and of course, the very heart of that room was the cast iron cook stove. Never absent from the stove top was the tin coated copper tea kettle from which we poured a pan of hot water for hand washing. In summer, I always found a left over ros'near or two, in fall or winter, there were sweet potatoes keeping soft and warm in the warming oven. And of course, there sat the wood box under one window. "Gwen, make haste and go get me a arm load of wood."

Before being heated by the early morning fire, that room was so cold in winter that on occasion, ice would have formed in the water bucket.

If the kitchen was cold in winter, then the back porch could be likened to Lower Slobovia. Storm windows and doors had yet to be invented but the windows of this room were the forerunners of storm windows. They were hinged at the top, and could be raised and hooked to the ceiling in summer. Tables, chairs and washstands were moved out there as soon as warm weather appeared. During canning season temperatures in the kitchen were well over the 100 degree mark, so a meal on a screened in back porch was much more comfortable.

There were two rooms upstairs; one was a bedroom, the other more or less a storage room. Granny had inherited Uncle Lark's musical casket (music box) and it was shoved aside to that attic room. Jeanett Fain indicated that Granny probably didn't inherit it, if the truth were known that Daddy simply walked in Uncle Lark's house after he died and removed it from the premises. Be that as it may, I removed it from Granny's attic and brought it home with me. Inside the box is a bar with tuned teeth that are struck by pins so arranged on a revolving cylinder as to produce a certain tune. Since the handle was broken, I was required to rotate the cylinder manually, if I wished to hear the music. There are eight "aires" programmed on the cylinder and if I played the whole repertoire, I had whiskers all over my fingers. But it was worth it, to sit up there on a rainy day, hearing the falling rain as it harmonized with "Monastery Bells", La Paloma", or my favorite, "Home Sweet Home." That music box is well over one hundred years old and certainly hasn't been relegated to my attic. It's always been displayed prominently in any house we've ever lived in.

Granny and Grandad

Also in that room were rags, saved in anticipation of quilt making (and I don't know why, for she never made a quilt in her entire life,) old clothes, a big box of canceled checks and ledgers. There were also yards and yards of lovely ecru silk, brought home from the parachute factory, which had opened in Lexington at the beginning of World War Two. This was one of the first examples of government waste. The flooring in one end of that room was very unstable, shaking and groaning every time it was trod upon. I hardly ventured to that end of the room lest I fall through to the room below. (The Sky is falling.) I sure did have lots of hang-ups. I remember when Dad would park his car in front of their house, and then back down onto River Road to turn around, I was scared half to death that he was going to back all the way down the Bill Ev Hillside and I'd end up in one of "them hollers." I really do think he tried to see just how far he could go without getting stuck.

Every spring, almost without fail, someone would go outside and discover the yearly colony of termites. They moved from one room to the other, doing their destructive chewing and boring. First one side of the house and then the other. Perhaps a floor needed repair one spring, a wall the next spring. Grandad called them termanites. I remember one year when they ate through a leather suitcase that was left on the dining room floor. The increased activity of the hens was another indication they had arrived. If some old hen just happened to be fortunate enough to be around when the first few made their appearance, she wasn't smart enough to keep quiet. She had to broadcast it with loud contented clucks and soon the whole flock was running, squawking and pecking to share in the bounty. Dad was never able to eliminate them; they were permanent residents as long as the house was there.

At one end of the smokehouse was the rain barrel. We could usually find a few wiggle tails swimming about. Growing right by the rain barrel was a paw paw tree. The fruit from that tree was more or less thought of as being daddy's personal private stash. I didn't like paw paws or I'm sure I would have been caught eating a few. In the right hand corner of the front yard was a basement from a grocery store that Great Uncle Ligee had owned and operated for a very short time back in the early nineteen hundreds. A few years later, the store burned, leaving that 30 foot square hole in the yard. It was about four feet deep and that was one more place for Esther and me to climb in and out of.

Great Grandma House

Her name was Martha Jane Stinnett and she was born in 1849 to Lindsey Stinnett, Jr. and Emily Jane Fain Stinnett. She was married in 1866 to Benjamin James House and they were the parents of twelve children. One of those children was my Mommy Johns. Now I don't remember anything about Grandma House but through a bit of research and quizzing two older cousins, have managed to find out a few things of interest. To me, anyway. Anyone who had twelve children, and raised two more left by the death of a sister deserves to have something written about her. Their children were James William, Lindsey, Cordelia, Mary Elizabeth, Laura Belle, Frances, Samuel Dillard, Myrtie Ann, Alvin, Etta, Minnie and an infant daughter who died at the age of six months. The fact that she raised ten and most all lived very long lives says something for the genes in that family. Uncle Lenny lived to be over a hundred years old, Aunt Minnie was in her nineties when she died and Mommy Johns was eighty-nine. James died of typhoid fever at the age of thirty-one and Etta died in her early teens. All the House girls were very attractive young women and Etta was a beautiful young girl. Mother gave me an antique picture frame that contained three pictures. I removed all of them to insert one more to my own liking and what a treasure I found. There was a portrait of a beautiful young lady and when I asked Mother her name, she said "Why, that's my Aunt Etty." I later learned that her family called her "Little Etty." Mother had also given me an ancient Gospel Primer. I displayed it at Christmas time with other old books and toys but had never looked beyond the first few pages. This year, when I picked it up to store it away, it fell open to the middle of the book and there was a yellowed, brittle obituary. It was little Etty's. It was 96 years old. Back in those days, all obituaries, wedding announcements and any newspaper article that contained a family name was clipped from the paper and usually placed in the family Bible. Since this was found in this Gospel Primer, I'm sure the book belonged to little Etty. This is the printed style of the 1896 obituary.

> Miss House's Death
>
> The fourteen-year-old daughter of Mr. and Mrs. Ben House, Miss Etta, died last Sunday morning of consumption. The funeral was From the residence and burial at the home place near Pink. The parents have the sympathy of all citizens.
> She was a sweet child and had many friends to mourn her death. Her last days were her happiest, Though she suffered a great deal; but all with a smile on her face. She went to sleep never to awake smiling. She left a bright testimony, said Jesus and his angels were coming for her. She prayed that he might take her out of her misery and He did. Her request was for the family and everyone to meet her in Heaven.

Grandma House was a very devout Methodist and with her husband, belonged first to the Pleasant Hill Methodist Church. They and their young children rode horseback to Sunday school and Church. After Pleasant Hill was sold and torn down, they became members of Mt. Beulah Church.

She was known for her salt rising bread, which she shared with her neighbors. I'd be willing to bet that it wasn't any better than grannies but no one will ever know because I never tasted either product. ("Ay, I couldn't go that salt rising bread.") Grandma House never wore any colors except gray or black or a combination or gray and white checks or black and white checks. She always wore an apron, even to church; her hats, purse and shoes were black. It was said that she wore an apron to church because she did not want the Lord to think she was proud.

She lived near Aunt Minnie and Uncle Larkin and when they became ill during the 1919 influenza epidemic, she stayed with them and cared for their children. She cooked mush and overdid it a bit for their daughter, Robin, said she had never eaten another bite of mush. For this generation's information, mush is cornmeal poured slowly into rapidly boiling water, cooked until done, then poured into loaf pan until it's cooled and set. It is then sliced, fried, and served with some kind of syrup. Sounds like something that's not done in the middle to me. (A little note here to my children. See how lucky you were, I never made you eat mush, souse, brains and eggs, dumplings and for sure I never cooked liver! All I did was tell you to eat your vegetables and drink your milk, so I wouldn't have any rickety grandchildren.)

Back to Grandma House. One of her daughters, Mary Elizabeth, (Aunt Lizzy) married Grandad's brother, Uncle Elijah Comley. That's really some confusing kinship line there, I never tried to analyze that, and I only know that everyone who is kin to them is kin to us. Anyone who wishes to figure that one out is welcome to have at it.

Anyway, they had five children, Virgie, Valerie, Oscar, Nela, and another daughter, whom they chose to name Etta. This was in memory of Aunt Lizzie's little sister, who died of consumption. Sadly enough, this Etta also died. She was only six years old.

Nela married a man named Chester Bain. She met him while riding a bus to work and Aunt Lizzie didn't like him. She told a few people in the family that Nela got on the wrong bus. Maybe so, but Nela and Chester produced the only child in that family. He was named Billy but was always called Billy Bain. Uncle Ligee and Aunt Lizzie would keep him for days. He was the pride and joy of the whole family, so you can imagine their despair when they learned he died from an aneurysm while studying at Johns Hopkins University Medical Center.

Nela, the only survivor, is in her nineties and Billy Bain and her immediate family are about all she remembers. On a recent trip to Lexington, I went to see her, and about every five minutes, she'd say, now you're Dola's girl, I always liked Calvin, then, did I show you this picture of Billy Bain? And she'd take it from the mantel, hand it to me for my admiration, then, now you're Dola's girl, etc. About 6 months later, I called her and she didn't remember our visit or that I was Dola's girl.

After their store burned, Great Uncle Ligee and Great Aunt Lizzie bought a house in Lexington and made that their permanent residence. By this time, their son, Oscar had opened a store in Nicholasville, called "Comley's Grocery." Uncle Ligee worked for him until he retired.

My mother, Mommy Johns and I made a trip to Lexington to visit Aunt Lizzie after they left Pollard. Now, back in those days, when nature called, and someone had to leave the room, it was called having to go outdoors. So after we had visited with Aunt Lizzie, admired the indoor bathroom and all the conveniences of city living, Mother asked her how she liked her new place. She replied that everything was terribly expensive, and remarked that it even cost you money to go outdoors. No one in Pollard had to pay a water bill.

Esther and I thought Aunt Lizzie was a real aristocrat because she lived in Lexington. That is, until one summer she came back to Pollard during blackberry picking time and Esther and I went to the blackberry patch to help her. After all the buckets were filled to the top, Aunt Lizzie remarked, "Well, I should have brung more buckets." Even Esther and I knew better than that, for whoever heard of an aristocrat saying brung?

Alvin House, Benjamin House and Martha Jane House

Superstitions, Signs and Omens

Since scientists had yet to discover the world of genetics, or if they had, Pollard folks were unaware of any such phenomena, certain traits ran in families. For example, extreme frugality ran in Mommy Johns' family. ("Sniff") Mother was convinced that suicide ran in a certain Pollard family. She could cite about seventeen instances of suicide down that line as proof positive. Since no one back then had ever heard of manic depression, there was no explanation other than the fact that it ran in that family.

Twins run in our family. There were Aunt Vina and Uncle Harry's girls, Ruth and Esther. Great Aunt Myrtie and Uncle Arch Hager were the parents of Buddy and Taydie. Uncle Homer and Aunt Hazel had Bobby and Betty. Then Lilburn Fain, son of Aunt Minnie and Uncle Larkin, and his wife Rose were blessed with two. In Aunt Vina's family, one of her grandchildren has twins and last but not least, Cherry presented us with our own Robert and Aaron.

Granny listened in on every conversation at the store and always observed each customer's purchases. One of her nieces came to our house once, and seeing a dress hanging on the wall, walked up and smelled under the armpit to see if it was new or if someone had passed it down to mother. Mother and I laughed about that for years. Cleanliness was another trait that ran in the Fain family. They were fanatics about cleanliness – not a speck of dirt in their house or on their person.

People also referred to families as having certain streaks. Such as that family has a mean streak.

If a baby happened to be born with a birth defect, it was not the result of a flaw in the genetic make-up, but was marked by something the mother had seen, dreamed, or heard. Everyone immediately started backtracking the pregnancy to recall any unusual event that might have occurred. I remember a baby being born with a very dark birthmark on its leg. If one stared long enough, one could see the nebulous outline of a horse's head. Someone told that the mother had witnessed a horse being brutally beaten by its owner and this resulted in the baby's being "marked." A simple strawberry birthmark was always the cause of much speculation about what the mother had seen during the pregnancy. And when that baby finally arrived, God forbid letting a cat get anywhere near it's little face. Everyone knew that cats would sneak up in a baby's face and suck the breath out of its little lungs.

My Mother would have a dream one night, then several days later something would occur to remind her of that dream and she always said, "Well. That's the end of my dream."

If we had a dream during the night and told someone about it before breakfast, it was supposed to come true. So if we had a pleasant dream, we hastened to tell it before breakfast. If we had a nightmare, our lips were sealed.

Uncle Herbert had brought a defunct coal oil water heater from his property and dumped it behind one of Mommy Johns' outbuildings. Grandpa Johns had been ill for some time and the family knew that he would never recover. Every afternoon about four o'clock. that water heater started making a loud thumping noise. They immediately assumed that the noise was a sign that Grandpa's time had come. Well, it had, but that thumping noise had nothing to do with it. Even at the early age of ten, Vic had an inquisitive and scientific mind. He started observing the heater and listening to the "THUMP! THUMP!

He concluded that the heat from the sun was making it expand and contract. When he reported that phenomenon to the adults, they were highly indignant. That was a sign and that was all there was to it. He was never able to convince them otherwise.

Mommy Johns always planted her garden crops by the sign of the moon. I heard her talk about setting onion slips by the sign and sowing seed potatoes during a certain phase of the moon and I looked at her Almanac but had absolutely no idea what it meant.

Another one of her superstitions had to do with dropping her dishrag. If she dropped the dishrag, that meant she was going to have company. Back then, we didn't have dishcloths, we had dishrags. They had to be used for something because nothing was thrown away. It didn't really mean she was going to have company; it merely meant the dishrag got a little dirtier.

There have been several things in this life that I've always wanted, but never had. One was natural curly hair, another a voluptuous figure and a fine singing voice. Well, we all know where I get my curls, I never had enough nerve to have a boob job, and I couldn't carry a tune in a bucket. But I could whistle! When I'd walk around those hilly roads with my lips puckered, I'd whistle a happy tune. Then as soon as I hit the front porch at Granny's house, she would say, "A whistlin' woman and a crowin' hen will come to a no good end." I don't know about that crowing hen, but I think I've done pretty well and I intend to continue to do good until the end.

Another superstition involved mourning doves. When we heard that low sound from some far away tree, we knew that a rain was coming our way. And we were told that if a turtle got a "holt" of our thumb, it would never let go until it heard a big clap of thunder. And of course there was always one of the uncles around at watermelon time to warn us against swallowing a watermelon seed, for just as sure as we did, we'd have a watermelon vine growing out of our nose.

High School

It was 1940, and after eight years in a two-room schoolhouse, I was going to Nicholasville High School. Ready or not, here I come! I was ready on Monday, not ready on Tuesday. Ready on Wednesday, not ready on Thursday. It was such a culture shock that on one day I'd feel as out of place as a harlot in church, while on the next day, I'd tell myself that those town girls put their panties on one leg at a time, just like I did.

While riding the bus the eight miles or so to Nicholasville, I was still in my element, for the rest of the kids on the bus were as country as I. With, perhaps, the exception of a few upper classmen, who had a year or two in which to shed some of the rawness and develop a certain degree of sophistication.

Nicholasville High School was a two story red brick structure with many classrooms; each with its separate cloakroom that was as long as the class room to which it belonged. The upstairs hall was so large that Pollard School could have been placed in the middle. (A bit of poetic license here and there adds to any story.) Imagine having a separate gymnasium! And a library with shelves of books lining every wall! I resolved to read every one of those books before I graduated and Lord knows, I tried. No more reading Elsie Dinsmore. Some of those books even had vague references to sex! We knew immediately which books had dirty passages-all that was required was to let the book fall open of its own volition and there it was. Most of us still knew very little about sex and those passages were read again and again.

No more carrying lunch (high school students didn't say dinner when referring to the noon meal.) We were privileged to go the cafeteria, pick up a tray, and select from meats, jello salads and vegetables. Everything looked better than it tasted. Some of the town kids who lived within walking distance went home for lunch. I longed to sneak down to the drugstore for one of those good hamburgers but I had neither the nerve nor the time.

One of the greatest adjustments to high school was having a different classroom for each subject. And can you believe having a different teacher for each subject? Of course the hub of all those different classrooms was homeroom. There was so much to remember! There was also the huge auditorium where assembly was held, guest speakers had their captive audiences, bands and choirs performed and the senior class had their senior play.

One of the most conscientious teachers was Mr. Tabb, who taught algebra. But not to me. When he stood at the blackboard with chalk in hand, and talked about X to the nth power or whatever, my eyes glazed over and I never heard a word he said. In today's society, I would be diagnosed as having attention deficit disorder and treated accordingly. I flunked algebra! If passing algebra was a requirement for graduation, and I'm sure it was, I would still be staring at that blackboard except for a quirk of fate.

As luck would have it, Mr. Tabb found a more lucrative position and Mrs. Hart was hired to take his place.

Mrs. Hart's knowledge of algebra was almost as scant as mine, but she was Miss Hattie Warner's widowed sister and she was in need of a job. Miss Hattie was The Principal. By this time I had become friends with Geraldine Sloan who lived directly across the street from Miss Hattie. Geraldine and I became quite adept in the art of apple-polishing and that's how I passed algebra. That would never have worked with Mr. Tabb. In all the many years since, never have I felt the urge to solve an algebra problem, and I'm sure that if I had to make the attempt, I'd get that same glazed look in my eyes.

Then there was Mrs. Lucille Hare, a gifted English teacher. Mrs. Hare exuded gentility, kindness and was greatly loved by all. No glazed eyes in her classes. When she read poetry, everything came to life. I even enjoyed diagramming sentences. I learned the meaning of onomatopoeia by listening as she recited Poe's "The Bells." I learned present tenses, past tenses and future tenses. But I've forgotten most of it. We studied reflective pronouns and intensive pronouns. I wince when I hear some sports analyst say, "There are spike marks between he and the hole." And he has my sympathy for I know that he didn't have a Mrs. Hare for high school English.

Miss Mattie Mae Glass' official title was librarian, but she was also called upon to lend a bit of international culture to those of us who wished to learn a Romance Language. I chose French. I somehow managed to pass two years of French, and I have retained the ability to do a small (very small) amount of translation. However, I was very poor at pronunciation; I lacked the ability to twist my tongue around those unfamiliar sounds.

Miss Glass, as did the other teachers, also presided over study hall. Study hall was in the library and to me, that meant reading, not studying.

Mr. Mullins was the attendance officer and coach. I had never played basketball before and I took to that game like a duck to water. We didn't have girl's teams that were affiliated with the school. We played basketball in physical education class and played softball when we could get enough girls together to make a team. I loved anything to do with sports and soon I decided that I would like to become a physical education teacher.

Reigning supreme over the Nicholasville High School faculty and the entire student body was Miss Hattie Warner. I couldn't have been more frightened of Lizzie Borden. Miss Hattie was tall, (probably not as tall as I remember her) ramrod straight and so tightly corseted that, when walking through the halls, nothing moved except arms and legs. Bad hair must have "run in" that family, for she and Mrs. Hart were the original models for whom the phrase, "I'm having a bad hair day." was coined. Both "do's" were similar, combed back, twisted at the back of the neck, then wound around the head and held in place by strategically placed hair pins. It was then fluffed and spread apart to cover an area of bare scalp here and there.

It was rumored all through my four years of high school that Miss Hattie wore a wig. I, for one, didn't want to get close enough to find out.

She was a strict disciplinarian who had no qualms about assigning "lines." I've seen her march down a crowded hall, holding some beefy football player by the ear while students scattered, leaving a path similar to the parting of the Red Sea. No one messed with Miss Hattie. When my cousin, Ima Jeanett, was a freshman, a few girls cooked up a scheme to skip school and ride the Phillips' bus to Lexington and spend the day at Joyland Park. Of course, Miss Hattie found out and called Uncle Irey. That was the last of her education until after World War II. When she reached the age of 18 she joined the Marines. At the end of the war she went back to school, graduated and also got a teaching certificate.

All of this completely overwhelmed a country girl from Pollard. I had absolutely no social graces - how could I, when no one in my family had any either. Not only was I ignorant, freckle faced, and definitely not a Miss America, I had to follow in the footsteps of a very handsome, intelligent and popular older brother, who had already graduated. He would have completely ignored me, even if he hadn't graduated, for I was somewhat of a smart aleck and every time I saw him with some girl, I always made some silly gesture or remark. I know that those juniors and seniors couldn't possibly believe that I was Victor Comley's little sister.

However, being unknown was nothing new to me. Occasionally, on our Saturdays spent in Nicholasville, Mother and I ran into someone whom she had not seen for a few years. I would receive a blank look and she would say to mother, "Why, Dola, I didn't know you had a girl." This has followed me all my life. First, I was Victor Comley's little sister. Then I married and my husband was successful, so I was introduced as Bill Lentz's wife. When our oldest daughter, Robin, was going to Lone Oak High School, she joined every organization that was offered and became very popular, so I was known as Robin Lentz's mother. Now my granddaughter, Beth, has won many contests and has her name in the local newspaper at least once a month, so therefore, I am known as Beth Lentz's grandmother.

But my time is coming. I am about to arrive. When I get this little story published and I am invited to appear on Oprah, I will have come into my own, and Vic will be forced to say, "I am Gwen Comley Lentz's big brother."

When I was a freshman at Nicholasville High School, I tried to copy the city kids. Mother still enjoyed sewing, so I had an adequate wardrobe. The economy was on the upswing in anticipation of World War Two and Daddy had an Honest to God job!

What I sadly lacked was grace and poise. I started watching the teachers so as to emulate their behavior. I noticed how they held their knives and forks; they took small bites and chewed their food thoroughly.

One minute I'd act like a town girl-the next minute I'd be walking with downcast eyes - on the alert for black hen doins'. On Monday, I'd realize how socially inept I was; on Tuesday, I'd be in a state of oblivion about who I was and where I came from. Lord, I wouldn't be fifteen years old again for anything.

When I became a High School student, I soon realized that there was more to life than a six-room house in Pollard. At Grandpa Milford's death Granny had heired, (that's country talk for inherited) considerable acreage in Pollard. On one lot catty-cornered from the store, stood a six-room house badly in need of paint or whitewash. Since Great Aunt "Idey" had inherited Grandpa Milford's house, we were forced to move. I was ten years old when we moved into that corner house. During grade school, I was oblivious to its appearance, although I'm sure many people observed it's gray weathered poplar siding and remarked, "They're too poor to paint and too proud to whitewash." Whitewash is a mixture of lime and water that is very inexpensive. That house had only one closet, but it was not for hanging clothes. There were two or three shelves and no real floor except several layers of linoleum and I enjoyed taking my books in there and reading. Wonder why I never thought of spiders. In the front room was a cabinet Victrola that Daddy had brought home from an auction. The former owner's taste in music was rather highbrow and all of those heavy 78 rpms were operas and Strauss waltzes. I'd sit in there, crank that Victrola and listen to that stuff for hours. Mother was as nervous then as I am now and I don't know how she could bear it. I don't even know why I listened to them for I knew nothing about opera and still don't.

No one had lawns-they had yards and ours was mostly weeds and was seldom mowed-maybe one or two times a summer.

Great Uncle Ira, Aunt Annie and their children lived just across the hill and every hot summer night they gathered out on their front porch (which faced the room where I slept) and started their nightly serenade. It also started their dogs howling. Of course, my window had to be kept open in case any little breeze came through and I could never get to sleep until they stopped singing. It would have been entertaining, had the dogs stayed quiet, but they couldn't carry a tune in a bucket and that is why I've always hated to hear a barking dog.

Until High School, I thought nothing about living there. Most people in Pollard were more destitute than we, and if the truth were known, I considered Granny's and Grandad's house my residence anyway and it was painted white.

We've all heard the expression, "How the Other Half Lives" and never was it brought to my attention more forcefully than when I observed the red brick or white clapboard houses in Nicholasville where my High School acquaintances lived. This was probably one of the most painful periods of my life. I day dreamed constantly; was hopelessly in love with one of Victor's friends who lived in a caretaker's house on one of the local horse farms. I pictured myself in a beautiful pair of dark green jodhpurs, riding on one of those high stepping mares. Of course, it bolted, ran away with me, and I was rescued just as my horse was ready to jump one of those white painted fences. As he held me in his arms, he realized how much he loved me and -POP-, "Gwen, go get me a bucket of water from the well." Back to reality!

That house was 150 years old, but the historical background, if any, completely escaped me. I remember standing in the front door when I saw a strange car coming up the road and I was so afraid it was some of my high school acquaintances that I ran back inside so I wouldn't be seen. It was highly unlikely that any of those town kids would be driving around Pollard, but I certainly didn't want to be seen in one of the most run down houses in the area. Also Jimmy Moore was the only person fortunate to have a car and he had no idea where Pollard was.

This was where I spent my teen years and it was almost as if I led two lives. A town life and a country life. The country life always overshadowed the town life. I didn't belong in the city and I didn't want to belong in the country. I only know that I felt so different from the other girls. There was Peggy Taylor, whose mother always welcomed all the kids with lemonade and cookies. Peggy talked of the good times she and her mother had, how close they were, but I never felt that I could talk to my mother about anything.

Then there was Mary Esther Brumfield, who lived in a nice little stucco house; had a father who was a judge, had three brothers, and they seemed to have so much fun as a family.

I met Bettye Lee Mastin and although we were as different as night and day, we entered into a friendship that lasted all through High School. Bettye Lee was a serious student who strived for A's, and I was a lazy student who was more interested in boys than grades. I was content with a B or C. Bettye had five sisters. That was a houseful, but there was always room for one more and I was always made to feel welcome. Her mother, Miss Ruby, was the Rose Kennedy of that clan, and like the parable of the fishes, could always add a cup of water to the stew or soup and feed a few more girls. Bettye Lee, Geraldine and I were very good friends, and had wonderful times together. Living in the country became much more bearable after Geraldine and I became close friends. One weekend she would come home with me and the next, I stayed in town with her. She didn't mind the inconveniences. We washed our hair in rainwater because we knew that made it shine more that washing it in town water.

In 1943 we were listening to the local news on the radio and learned that the Nicholasville High school building had burned to the ground. Well, thank God for Miss Hattie. She found a large vacant house on south Third Street. Those of us who had not enrolled at University High in Lexington went to classes as usual although so much had changed. We had no Library. We were even short-handed for school books. At this time, the boys on the football team and the basket ball team voted for the cheerleaders. I was much honored to be selected although I was fairly sure that I would never have made if some of the more popular girls had not finked out and graduated from U.Hi. I have never had a good sense of rhythm and it's a good thing the exercises were rather simple. Just had to yell Two bits, Four bits, Six bits a dollar-all for Nicholasville, stand up and Holler. Then we walked up and down past the fans and clapped while yelling Siss Boom Bah - All for Nicholasville, Rah Rah Rah.

Every graduating class had a senior play. And since the house had no stage, Miss Hattie somehow managed to borrow the court house and that's where we had Class night. And Senior play. Ours was called Never Say Die. I was "Estelle" and I wore a blue dress with a white organdy apron – don't remember the significance of that apron. It's possible that was a fad then. Mother had made the outfit and of course, I thought I was hot stuff. And speaking of fads, a teen aged girl's wardrobe was totally incomplete without a pink, pale blue or white angora sweater. They were really pretty but shed like a long haired cat if you went to a dance and your date wore a dark suit.

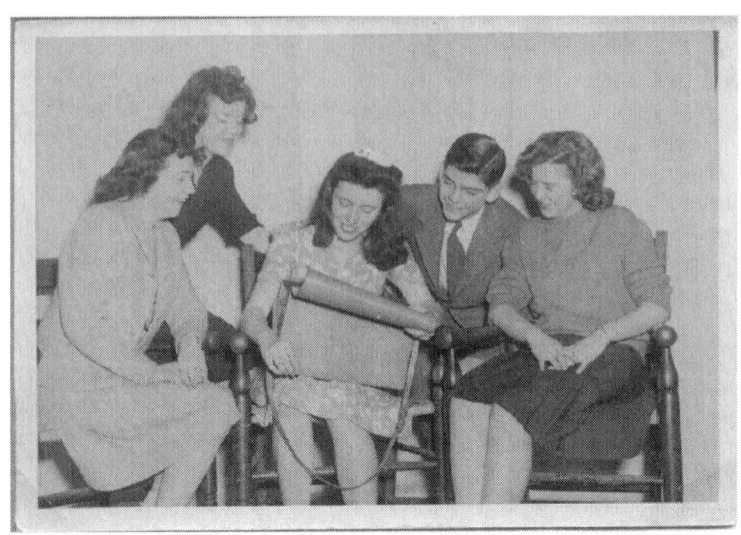

High School Play Photo – Geraldine Sloan Comley standing, Gwen Comley Lentz on far right

I was in love with the Methodist preacher's son and Bettye Lee was in love with his brother. Neither was in love with us! Geraldine was in love with so many that I can't remember their names and they were all in love with her. Several years later at a class reunion, Bettye Lee admitted to being relieved that God had not seen fit to grant her every prayer, for what on earth would she have done with that preacher's son had he suddenly materialized and said, Here I am, I'm all yours. I'll be the first to admit that I have felt the same relief that a few boys have not shown up on my front porch. God does work in mysterious ways.

Although I was beginning to feel a bit more comfortable with who I was and where I came from, there were two or three girls in Nicholasville High School, who were, to me, the ultimate in breeding and culture. They were quiet, lady like and everything I was not but aspired to be. I felt sure that if they had occasion to be seated in a formal dining room with six pieces of silverware on each side of the plate, they would have known instinctively which piece was used with each course. I was totally unaware that one of them was my second or third cousin. If she was aware that we were relatives, she never acknowledged that fact. They always wore plaid pleated skirts, white blouses with little Peter Pan collars, and saddle oxfords or penny loafers with the appropriate white socks. I haven't seen them for years, but I'll bet their present wardrobe is ordered from a Talbot Catalog.

All three of these girls lived in pretty houses on a tree-lined street in Nicholasville. One's father owned a hardware company, one's father was the only dentist in Nicholasville (and was actually a distant cousin, but I'm sure she wouldn't claim kin to me but would have Victor) and I never knew the third father's occupation.

However, there is more to education than is found in books and by observing, listening and remembering, I was learning. Actually, what I wanted to learn wasn't in books. I wanted to learn how to be like other girls. And I wanted to be popular.

I was beginning to feel a bit more acclimated to high school, my freshman year was behind me and a summer in Pollard loomed upon the horizon. I was happy to be free of history and algebra, but I was bored in the country. By this time, Esther had gone to live with her Mother in Cincinnati. That didn't last very long but she wasn't about to come back to Pollard. So she shared a rented room in Nicholasville and worked at the drugstore. This was a very painful period for Mommy Johns; for she had taken care of Esther for many years and she felt as if Esther were one of her own children. I'm sure she was her favorite grandchild. She seldom came back to Pollard and this was another heartache for Mommy.

Daddy was always buying a truckload of stuff from some auction and the summer of my fifteenth year, he brought home a silver Schwinn bicycle. Used, of course. But this was one of the few times that I can remember Mother and Daddy having fun together. Since she had grown up with five brothers, she had somehow learned to ride a bicycle. As he unloaded it, she wondered if she could still ride one. Somewhat in the way that I now wonder if I could still milk a cow. He bet her fifty cents that she couldn't ride it to the graveyard and back. This was a distance equal to two and a half city blocks. Since this was directly before she got religion and betting then became a sin, she rose to the challenge. She climbed on the bike, wibbled and wobbled about fifty yards until memory and balance kicked in and off she went. Thereby proving once again the theory that it's just like riding a bicycle, one never forgets. Upon reaching the graveyard, she turned around, pedaled back at break neck speed, and within a few yards of where we were standing, stopped with a flourish. He handed her fifty cents while I stood there dumb founded. My mother could ride a bicycle and I couldn't. However, I soon learned. Like most everything else he brought home, it was badly in need of repair. It had a raspy screech that heralded my impending arrival at least five minutes before my actual presence. Although there were only two of them instead of four, I had wheels! I no longer had to walk all over Pollard. To my knowledge, I was the only girl in Pollard who had a bicycle.

It was always exciting for Dad to come home from one of his all day trips to Lexington, although on occasion it was two or three days. We never knew what he'd have on the back of that truck nor would we know what level of inebriation he would have reached. Grandad had a perfect description. "Ay, he's about three thirds."

While I was struggling with high school, Vic was struggling with higher education. In fact, he had been struggling for two years. It's always been a source of amazement and admiration when I think about the hardships he had to overcome while getting a college degree. A small tobacco crop that he harvested in the fall of 1937 paid for the tuition for his first semester. Transportation was such a problem that he chose not to continue. And that's when Dad came up with one of the few words of wisdom that he ever gave either one of us. He asked Vic if he was going back to school and when he answered no, Dad said, "Well, I don't know what you think you're going to amount to down in these hills." Those few words ignited a fire that was not quenched until four years later when he graduated from the University of Kentucky.

Bob Butler worked in Lexington at the Stanley Fizer Plumbing and Heating Company and was required to be on the job at seven o'clock in the morning. He was only too happy to have Vic share a ride to Lexington. His first class didn't start until eight, and he had become friends with a Sergeant Mcdaniels, who unlocked a side door and Vic studied until "books took up." That semester's tuition was paid for with the proceeds from a small crop of tobacco. Since Bob and Vic's timing seldom agreed in the afternoon, he was more often than not reduced to hitch hiking or walking. Finding a ride from Lexington to Nicholasville was fairly easy, but he often had to walk at least part of the way from Nicholasville to Pollard. Uncle Wilbert had bought a 1930 roadster, which he was unable to drive, but O'Dell could, and two or three times, they drove right on by as Vic was walking to town. Uncle Wilbert made the statement that Vic "didn't need no education, he ort to be out workin' like the rest of us." And Dad's first cousin owned his own car and was also attending U.K. Grandad offered to pay him to swing 'round through Pollard so Vic could ride with him. But his Mother said "No, if he didn't have money, then he didn't need to be trying to go to school." Now, one might wonder why Dad, who always, and I do mean ALWAYS, had some means of transportation, didn't take him since, chances are, he was going anyway. Well, I don't know. But after Vic graduated someone remarked to Dad that Vic sure did have a hard time getting an education, and you know what he said? "Well, yeah, but it didn't hurt him none."

The War Years

Everyone of my generation remembers where they were in the late evening of December 7, 1941. I had been to some kind of church meeting, (probably Methodist Youth Fellowship) and as usual in the wintertime, was spending the night with Grandad and Granny. When I walked in, the radio was on, and they were listening to the news. On every station was the announcement that the Japanese had bombed Pearl Harbor. This meant that Vic who had joined the R.O.T.C. while attending college (earning twenty-five cents per day was his incentive for that) would soon be in the army and Lord only knows where he'd be sent. We didn't have to face that situation immediately, for he was granted a deferment until June of 1942, when he graduated as a 2nd Lieutenant. At that time, I really couldn't grasp the horror of war, but I was afraid because all of the adults were so afraid. And of course, that was perfectly natural for me because I'd been scared ever since I was eight years old and Uncle Roland had told me there were bears in them hollers.

As soon as Vic graduated, he received orders to report to Camp Edwards, Massachusetts. Although we had known this was inevitable, it was a very sad time for all of us. After Vic had told Granny goodbye, he walked down to the car so Dad could drive him to Lexington where he to be transported by bus to Massachusetts. As they backed out of the barn lot out onto the road, Vic looked back and there stood Grandad, wearing his old felt cowboy hat and he was crying. That image was etched in his memory forever; he still talks about it to anyone who will listen. And of course Mother was devastated. I swore I'd write to him every day and I almost did, although there were times when I had to fabricate a story or two, just to have something to write about. Bettye Lee had a vivid imagination and occasionally when the source of news was as dry as a bone yard, she and I would put our heads together and write something that we thought was comical. That came to a screeching halt when Vic wrote back that he was tired of that foolishness and wanted Pollard news.

Six weeks after basic training at Camp Edwards, he called the store and asked someone to run up to our house and tell Mother she had a phone call from Victor. That was how we learned he was going overseas. School was out for the summer and I happened to be home. She came back up the road crying, and fell face down on the bed, and I heard a muffled, anguished "I'll never see him again." I remember that as well as if it was yesterday, but that's all I remember. I know that I was more shocked at the way she was acting than I was that Vic was going "across the waters" as Grandad said. That was the first time I had ever seen her cry, and I had no idea how to comfort her. She found a way though and it was through religion. Her Bible collected no dust from then until her death.

We knew firsthand what patriotism was; children collected tin foil from chewing gum and discarded cigarette packages. It was rolled into balls and saved for the war effort. It was melted and used in shipbuilding. Hardly a store window escaped displaying a cardboard picture of Uncle Sam, wearing his top hat of red, white and blue, his long flowing white beard, proud symbol of the United States, pointing a finger at every passerby and saying I WANT YOU. Young men enlisted, young men were drafted and a few young men became conscientious objectors and were impounded in an enclosure in Arizona.

So many were killed, blown to bits or wounded and left to die on battlefields, ships were torpedoed and sunk while a few survivors clung to life surrounded by death and near death and wondering if they would ever see their loved ones again. The best way to describe the loss of a beloved brother is to copy directly from letters written to me from my cousin Morrison Davis' sister -Lucille and the remaining brother, Paul.

"We were a very close family with eleven children born in fourteen years. We knew one another very well. We worked, played and prayed together. When the telegram arrived in November 1943 saying the Liscome Bay had been sunk and Morrison was missing in action we were devastated. I clearly remember my father standing at the end of the piano where Morrison's picture stood praying and crying "God take me, let my son live if it's your will." This I saw for several days at various times. Day or night. I remember my mother lying on the couch in the living room--with her heart broken. Just to see my mother lying down in the daytime was most unusual.

Every night during family prayers (for years) Daddy continued to pray, "Oh God, if Morrison is on some island, keep him safe until he is found. After I married and would return home to visit, they both still prayed for his safe return. His National Service Life Insurance was used to start the Nazarene Church in Fayetteville, Arkansas. From my own perspective, I couldn't accept or believe the facts. He lived with Uncle Herbert and Aunt Mayme for a year in Nicholasville and dated one of the local high school girls. When he came home at the end of the school year, Daddy let him use the few acres west of our house to raise beans to earn his own money. I picked beans for him but earned very little because the crop was so poor. He played football in the front yard on Sunday afternoon with a lot of boys from town. I used to iron his white shirt before he left for a date with a girl friend. We were such good friends. My bedroom was downstairs, next to the living room wall where the piano sat and I know the tears and prayers of Mother and Daddy for his safe return. I recall every movie that I went to with a war theme (most of them were) I sat and cried. A good friend sat with me and held my hand. I never talked about him or what happened. It was much too painful. There was no such thing as grief counseling then. My brother, Eugene, was very close to Morrison. He and some of Morrison's friends took Daddy's car without permission and drove to see Morrison shortly after he joined the Navy. It was a Southern state, but I don't know where. Daddy was glad that they were able to see him but would have preferred giving permission first. Of all the children, I believe that Eugene was the most hurt by this tragedy. I haven't thought of all these details for some time and writing this brings back the sadness and reminds me again of how Mother and Daddy suffered and how hurt we all were."

And now for some words from another sister, Mildred.

"Morrison was so sweet. One night it was raining very hard. Our dog kept barking and wouldn't stop. Mother went to the stairs and called Morrison until he woke up and came down. She asked if he would get dressed and go outside with her and find out what was out there for the dog was a good guard dog. Morrison asked why she had asked him and she replied, 'I knew you were the only one who would go with me without fussing.' They found a big coat hanging on a post. When he lived with Uncle Herbert and Aunt Mayme that year he was on his way downtown on Saturday for he had earned four dollars for the week. He was going to buy a pair of shoes and go to the movies. He met a man on the street and as they talked he told Morrison that he had five children and had a chance to get a job but he had to have shoes--his were falling apart--Morrison gave him the four dollars and went home.

When he was in the Navy and stationed in California, just before he shipped out, he and three buddies came to see me. We had a picnic and sat around visiting and having fun and one teased Morrison and said, 'With such an impressive name, how could you have a face like that?' Morrison got a bigger kick out of the kidding than any of them. He had such a good natured disposition."

And now a few words from Paul.

"I have read in Naval History that the Liscome Bay was a ship that was called a cruiser and it was loaded with fuel and ammunitions. All explosives. When Japanese torpedoes hit it, it simply disintegrated, blowing completely to pieces. It sank in less than five minutes. Out of a crew of around 1,150 men, there were fewer than twenty-five survivors. These were men who happened to be on deck and were blown clear of the ship. This occurred near the Gilbert Islands."

This is a lot about to write about one person, but Morrison's death affected the whole family. I always read Aunt Vina's letters to my mother and for years, she would write, "Oh, Dola, my poor Morrison."

Young children learned to hate. They hated because adults hated. They hated the Germans; they hated the Italians and especially the Japanese because of the sneaky attack on Pearl Harbor.

President Franklin D. Roosevelt held fireside talks All of us knew President Roosevelt's words, "December, seventh was A day of infamy." And later, "We have nothing to feah except feah itself."

As soon as service men were in combat or in what was a classified area, they were required to use V-Mail stationery. This was government issued and was folded in a way that was easily opened to censors. Occasionally, certain phrases or sentences were cut out and then relatives knew that their loved ones were in the war zone. That old squeaky bicycle had a lot of mileage added to it during those years for just as soon as the mail came and there was a letter from Vic, we read it and I jumped on the bike and hurried to tell Granny and Grandad.

Teen-age girls turned up their noses at teen aged boys and fell in love with uniforms. We went out with boys we wouldn't have been caught dead with just because of that uniform. I went out with others but my heart really belonged to that friend of Victors who rescued me from the imaginary runaway horse. To be honest, certain uniforms appealed to some of us more than others, and Air Force Uniforms were favorites. Since they thought they had the most glamorous jobs in the war, it was passed on to impressionable young girls who didn't have the sense God gave a goose. Like me. And I knew I had two chances with him - slim and none. Let's be realistic and omit slim. But I did write to him and thought I was heartbroken when his plane was shot down, he was captured and spent the remainder of the war as a German prisoner of war. Just before he was captured, he had sent me a pair of silver wings like the ones worn on a pilot's uniform. And then came a letter saying he was waiting to marry a little girl from Kentucky or something like that. I called his mother, from the store and read the letter to her, thinking she would be elated for any news at all. Well, she might have been happy to know that he was still among the living, but that was about the coldest reception I ever had in my entire life. A country girl from Pollard was absolutely the last person she wanted for a daughter-in-law. She needn't have worried, I wore those wings pinned on everything but my gown and probably slept with them under my pillow, but that was the last time I ever heard from him. Or set my two eyes on him for that matter. When the war was over, he was released, sent home and I kept waiting and waiting and waiting. Then he married someone closer to his age and "station" and it wasn't long until I was in love with someone else. I never understood why he did that unless he thought he would never get out of that prison camp alive (so many didn't) and he might as well make some silly sixteen year old happy. Actually, I was having the time of my life, practically living with Geraldine's Aunt Ella and Uncle Jesse and away from Pollard.

Uncle Jesse was the first city mail carrier and the summer after I graduated from high school he saw to it that I had a job carrying mail also. Most of the able bodied young men were in the service and I was strong and had no problem slinging that leather backpack over my shoulder. In fact, I liked being a carrier. My route was through an area that was then known as Herveytown. I soon learned that not all blacks looked alike and after a week or so knew that route like the back of my hand. At noon I walked back to Aunt Ella's house and ate a big dinner then back to the post office to sort mail for the next day. Aunt Ella charged me two dollars a week for room and board. I can't remember exactly what my salary was, but it was more money than I had ever seen and I paid for a semester at U.K. It sure beat setting tobacco and picking off tobacco worms. I really liked city living, too. Taking a bath in a bathtub and not having to walk in a dirty barnyard. That was sort of the beginning of my leaving Pollard.

The economy was on the upswing, and any able bodied person could get a job. Airplanes, warships and submarines were being manufactured and factories were everywhere. Women were in demand for jobs other than teaching, nursing, and housekeeping. Detroit practically stopped car production and concentrated on shipbuilding. Ships were named for states and as they were completed they were anchored in some New York harbor. Celebrities christened the ships by breaking a bottle of champagne on the bow.

Rationing was not particularly new to us; if you had little money, then you didn't buy much. But this was different, money was available, but tires, gasoline, sugar, and many other things were not. Dad had a job at the parachute factory in Lexington. This was probably the easiest money he ever made, although backtracking a bit, when he brought those dirty, greasy mayonnaise jars from behind some Lexington restaurant and Vic and I had to clean them to sell, that wasn't too hard on him. I do believe he could think of more ways to make money than anyone I've ever known. But Mother was no slouch when money was to be had, either. While working at the redryer in Lexington, someone had shown her how to make artificial flowers from a material that felt remarkably like real petals. The materials were sold in kits complete with stems, leaves and five-inch squares of material. Instructions were quite explicit and with practice, Mother and Vic would have several corsages for sale every day. To quote an old saying, they sold like hotcakes. Then Dad had an even better idea. If they looked like roses, felt like roses, then they should smell like roses. Unfortunately, he had never stopped to smell the roses so he bought a bottle of Evening In Paris "colgeen" and not only did the flowers smell sweet, so did we.

One of the first countries Vic was stationed in was England. And of course those English girls liked uniforms as much as we did. Well...they really liked them a bit more than we did because of the added incentive of becoming a War Bride. A pretty, fair skinned, blonde English girl named Pat thought she had snared Vic. She wrote letters to us, sent glamorous photographs, but I was the one who answered the letters. Mother didn't think much of such goings on. I'm not saying that Pat liked Vic because of the uniform and because he was an American. He was a very handsome young man and really did cut a wide swath in that uniform. I'm sure he didn't have to use that old line, "I might be shot tomorrow, and wouldn't you feel badly if, etc, etc, etc." But he knew that he was coming back safe and sound and she wasn't going to become his English War Bride. For he had met Geraldine right before the war and after I sent him a picture of her he thought "I just might marry that little girl when I come home" and we all know that he did. And she is the best thing that ever happened to him: she and I were such good friends that we practically lived together. I could tolerate being in the country so much better when Daddy would bring us to Granny's and Grandads for the weekend. Both of them loved her, especially Granny. She had never in her life been teased and Geraldine was always saying funny things to make her laugh. She didn't care if we messed and gommed in the kitchen - we had to clean everything. We made mostly sea foam candy and a one egg yellow cake. Of utmost importance to us was getting a TAN. We were foolish enough to climb on top the porch, slather baby oil all over our bodies and burn. It was just like a sauna up there. We had some wild idea that the closer to the sun we were, the more we'd tan.

Granny and Grandad were both very fond of her. She would say something very funny and just a tiny bit off color and Granny had to grin and turn her head so we didn't see her. Grandad just sat there and went along with anything we did. I think Geraldine felt in her heart that she would probably marry Vic someday.

But Victor's being gone was not the only worry we had during the war years. Granny had always been the picture of health, seldom sick, was capable of doing everything required of a farm woman of that era, in fact, since Grandad was so crippled, she did more than most women. (Except Mommy Johns.) But when she began falling off (losing weight) and having terrible spells of back pain Mother and Daddy were beginning to prepare themselves to move in and take care of her. Dr. Williams performed surgery on her back and removed a baseball-sized tumor below her right shoulder. It was a cancer. Not cancer. A cancer. It was also a hush-hush disease. No one talked about a cancer. By the time the surgery was performed, it had metastasized, causing many other problems. If she had a three or four day and night bout of nausea and vomiting, she and Grandad said it was caused by something she had eaten and she would no longer eat that. Dr Williams was called, he gave her enough morphine to kill a horse and after about three days in bed, she was able to get up and do a bit of cooking and possibly even milk the cow. Then, still losing weight, she'd have another 'spell' for that was the accepted name for most illnesses. "So and So had a bad spell last night, we better go see if we can hep out a little." The summer before Mother and Daddy moved in to care for them, I was often sent to spend the night. I wasn't much for cooking but I could milk (I was thankful there was only one cow) and I didn't mind feeding chickens and bringing in a bucket of water for I had always done that. But being around a very sick person was almost more than I could handle.

I'm almost seventy-four years old and I've never forgotten the spell she had when I was sixteen and was staying there. If I live to be a hundred, I'll still remember, but can hardly write about it. She wasn't feeling well when she went to bed, but then she almost never felt well, but I could never have anticipated that Grandad would call me to get up and help. But there was nothing I knew to do. We took turns holding the slop jar so she could vomit, but there was no reason for that, because all that terrible heaving produced little for she had eaten nothing. All there was was pain, heaving and moaning. Finally, Grandad said, "Gwen, you'll have to go across the road and wake Roland and tell him to go get Calvin and Dola." I lit the lantern, went out the back screen door, careful not to run into the clothes line, past the hen house, where the hens shifted in their sleep, clucked nervously and settled back down, followed the path through what had once been the orchard, down to the gap between the hedges. My feet felt every little washout for I had walked that same path for years, but never in the middle of the night. I don't even remember knocking on Mommy's door but Roland hurried to our house by the store, called for Dad to get up and get dressed, then Garland, who lived right by the store opened up for Dad to call Dr. Williams. That was one night that Roland didn't mention bears and I didn't even think bears. The reason I don't remember knocking on Mommy's door because it was summer time and doors were wide open with only a screen door that might or might not be hooked.

I went back across the road, dreading with all my heart to being alone with them again and yet there was such a load being lifted to know that Mother and Daddy would soon be there. Dr. Williams always came when he was called, for he knew how badly he was needed. And he didn't fool around. As soon as he arrived, he gave her a shot of morphine that lasted about three days, he never hesitated; there was no danger of addiction, for country people never called a doctor unless they were critical. After that, I never had to stay by myself anymore.

I've always felt guilty because I was so frightened that I thought only of myself. That's a long time to allow such feelings to remain in the conscience of my mind. I have often wished I had a trap door to my brain and could destroy so many of the things that I dislike about myself. I try to turn back the pages of my life and look in the crevices of my brain and place the blame on the environment, or on the people who raised me, or on anything.

Mother and Daddy left the little house across from the store and moved in with Granny and Grandad.

I never heard my mother utter one word of complaint and I know that she was never close to her mother-in-law for their personalities were as different as Methodists and Campbellites. (Mommy Johns always said, "Them ol' camelites.") I'm sure and certain that Mother didn't keep house as well as Granny did, but on the other hand, I never heard Granny complain either. They were bonded together by so much need from the old folks, concern, deep pity, and awareness of duty from the younger generation, that not to have taken care of them never entered their mind.

Meanwhile, Victor was being sent from Ireland, to England, North Africa, Algiers, Tunisia, Naples, Marseilles, Alsace-Lorraine and was in Germany when the war ended. One interesting story occurred while he was stationed in a small village near Naples. There were always small children following the Americans, begging for food and cigarettes and even searching the garbage cans. One youngster about 16 years old showed up so frequently that he was unofficially adopted and was allowed to help around the kitchen. Vic and his good friend Vince Vangenees found a uniform for him and even gave him a PFC stripe, and for good measure they even named him Tony. When they moved into Germany, Tony moved along with his new friends. Of course this was unacceptable with the higher-ups and upon discovering what was going on, orders were issued to get rid of Tony. They took him to an airport in Naples and sent him back to Italy. Well you can't keep a good Italian down so he found his way back to Germany on his own, where he again met up with his benefactors. And there a man named Esposito adopted him, along with many other war orphans. That is one theory why there are so many "Espositos."

When Vic came home in September of 1945, he was shocked and dismayed to find Granny so thin and frail. She had always been "stout", but loss of appetite and back surgery combined had reduced a once healthy woman to a shadow of her former self. Nevertheless, she still knew her way around the kitchen. Mother, overwhelmed with excitement and nervousness at having him home was trying to fry a chicken, spattered grease all over herself and the stove said, "Well, I can't seem to get anything done." Granny said, "Well, move over and let me do it, I can still cook."

It's funny how little things like that stand out and I still remember them after so many years. I also remember that he couldn't sit down and relax, either. (Actually that wasn't so unusual, he never could be still, he didn't walk through the house but tap-danced from one room to the other.)

Only he knows how long it took for him to become acclimated to civilian life again; he and Daddy formed a closer relationship but he and Geraldine REALLY formed a close relationship. In fact, they were married on her birthday, June 22, 1946. Grandad was there with a tobacco stick in each hand, but Granny was unable to attend.

I was living in Lexington and sharing an apartment with my friend, Ruby Jean Fain. I have forgotten where I was working, but I would work awhile and go to U.K. awhile. One Friday, Daddy appeared in the doorway of the office (which in itself was unusual) and when I said, "Well, what are you doing here?" he told me to get my things and come on home. No "Hello." No reason, just "Get your things and lets go home." And when I told him I had already made plans for the weekend, He said, "Well, I guess you can change that and come on home, for your Granny's dead." Talk about Aunt Ida being behind the door when tact was passed out. Well, he was under the house. I was well aware that she was very sick and she was going to die at any time but that was a really terrible way of breaking the news to me.

That night, when it was time to go to bed, Mother looked at Grandad, getting ready to sleep by himself, and then she looked at me and said, "Gwen, honey, why don't you sleep with your Grandad tonight?" No one asked him how he felt but perhaps she sensed that he didn't want to be alone. I don't know, I just lay down on Granny's side and slept with him. Her funeral was held two days later and she was buried in the Fain graveyard near Uncle Ira's house.

Sex Education in the Thirties

HA! HA! And HEE! HEE! I considered leaving this chapter blank because there was no such thing as sex education. All I knew about sex was what I imagined when that handsome black haired man took that beautiful woman in his arms and True Story Magazine faded out until next month. And that didn't go any farther than kissing.

Esther and I discussed and wondered, and wondered and discussed where babies came from. We had a vague idea, but we knew that "doin' it" was a sin. Since Aunt Vina and Uncle Harry were certainly above reproach and never sinned, then there was no way that they would ever "do it." But how did they get all that gaggle of kids? We knew the other uncles would do most anything, but Uncle Harry was, to our minds, as pure as the driven snow. That certainly was a "puzzlement."

Somehow, somewhere Esther and I had heard the word "hermaphrodite" which sent us flying to the dictionary. Of course, we couldn't possibly find it because we didn't know how it was spelled. It was said that one of Grandpa John's sisters was married to one; she never had any children - neither did he.

I can never ever remember any adult giving me any information about sex, with the exception of Granny's oft repeated warnings that "Boys'll rairn ye." She spoke with a rapid delivery and all of her words seem to run together. "Boys'llrairnye." I had absolutely no idea what she meant. What could boys do to me? I could out run most of them. I could hold my own in a fight with any of them who were my size. I knew that if I asked her how a boy could rairn me, she would reply, "They just can." and that would be the end of that conversation. Whee, why, just why, that's why.

I later learned that she was telling me in a not too subtle way, that if I had sex before marriage, I would be "rairnt" and most likely couldn't get a husband. Because whoever "rairnt" me would be sure to tell all the other boys and no man wanted to marry a girl who was "rairnt." Not only would I not get a husband, but also I would get something that I didn't want and that something was a baby. I didn't even know anyone who had had to get married, or anyone who had an out of wedlock child. Back then, that was such a disgrace.

Later in high school and college, I fell in and out of love with several different boys. Whenever I was tempted to stray from the straight and narrow or when I heard that old line, "If you really loved me, you would." Or that really pitiful one, "I'll probably be sent to Italy or France next week and I'll be over there fighting for my country and don't you want me to go "across the waters" with pleasant memories?" Yeah, right! But there was always that voice in one ear that said, "Boys'llrarnye, boys'llrarnye." And if I said, "Go away, this is a nice boy that I'm in this back seat with." Then it instantly appeared in the other ear "BOYS'LLRAIRNYE!" She certainly did a number on me.

I never observed the sexual activity of many of the farm animals. Cats had their liaisons at nighttime and their eerie howling was an indication that something was happening. Dogs doing their business were downright dirty and hens and roosters having sex was something to laugh at. Roosters were so funny; they always strutted around the hen sideways several times, jumped on top, pecked her comb, (I wondered if he held onto her comb to avoid falling) then got off, fluffed his feathers and strutted away in search of another Dominecker hen. I always thought if a rooster could talk he would say, "Look at me! Look at me!" And when Viagra was discovered, it surely was made possible by some man observing the goings on in the chicken yard.

I was so naive that I'm sure I was in the tenth or eleventh grade before I finally learned the facts of life and it was probably Geraldine who educated me. I do know that those were the days before "The Pill" and the fear of an unwanted pregnancy was enough for most of us to keep our legs crossed.

Great Aunts and Uncles

Uncle Wilbert was Grandad's brother; therefore he and his wife, Agnes, were mine and Vic's Great Uncle and Great Aunt. Since they lived less than a mile away, we frequently visited back and forth. Granny's and Grandad's house was the first house on Kissin' Ridge Lane and Uncle Wilbert and Aunt Agnes lived less than a mile past our house. They had only one son; his name was Odell Lee. My mind is a total blank when trying to recall Uncle Wilbert's features, but I can conjure up an instant image of Aunt Agnes. She was a small, sharp-faced little woman and like all women of that time and age wore her hair pulled back in a bun or biscuit at the back of her neck. Her print dresses were always below mid-calf and her dirty, skinny little legs seemed to have sprouted and grown from a pair of aged grungy tennis shoes. The three of them worked constantly at any job that enabled them to earn money. Nothing was too menial, too degrading or too difficult. They owned a large farm on Kissin' Ridge and also considerable acreage of rich river bottom land. Their sole purpose in life was to work and earn money. The latter being the result of the former. In fact, their work ethic was so strong, so ingrained; that they felt everyone should work as hard as they. When Vic was attending U. K., he started walking the eight miles to Nicholasville. Usually, someone came along and offered him a ride. Back in those days, most everyone fortunate enough to own a car always stopped to pick up any pedestrian. One morning, when Vic was about half way to Nicholasville, he heard a car and turning around, saw that it was Uncle Wilbert and Aunt Agnes. They drove right on by. By that single act, they stated that it was their opinion that Victor had enough education and it was high time he stopped all that foolishness and started working on those hillsides. Comleys don't hold a grudge though and our relationship with them continued as if nothing had ever happened.

Uncle Wilbert would visit Grandad and ask if we had tomatoes yet. Or beans or corn or whatever. And if Grandad said, "No, ours ain't come in yit." Uncle Wilbert always said, "Sy, uffin Ida knowed ye didn't have none, Ida brung ye some." Now when I go to Nicholasville, I always tell Vic that uffin Ida knowed he didn't have no Western Kentucky barbecue, Ida brung him some.

Odell married a lovely girl from Poozy Ridge, which is located in Madison County and is right across the river. Her name was Doreen and she had the most beautiful smile in Pollard. They lived with Aunt Agnes and Uncle Wilbert and every day, when the men went to the fields, Doreen and Aunt Agnes went with them. She planted tobacco, she hoed corn, she canned vegetables, and she picked blackberries to be sold in town. It was as if Odell had brought her into that family for the purpose of adding more money to their already ample bank account. They had no children, but then Uncle Wilbert and Aunt Agnes weren't very prolific either.

Doreen was allowed to visit her family in Madison every weekend. One Saturday, as usual, Doreen packed only a change of clothing and a toothbrush for that beautiful smile. With no regrets, she then walked to the river where she boarded the ferry, rode across the river never to return. She and Odell had been married fifteen years; she had worked from daylight until dark five days a week and she had absolutely nothing, with the exception of a change of clothing, a toothbrush and a great sense of relief. She stayed with her family until finding employment in Lexington where she lived for many years. She never remarried.

Aunt Agnes did ask her what she wished to inherit in the event of her death - land or money. Doreen replied, "Whatever you want to give me." She never received anything, because when Aunt Agnes died she didn't have a will.

Like many other Pollard residents, Uncle Wilbert and Aunt Agnes were far too frugal to spend money on any medical treatment. Once, he had some ailment so painful that he was forced to see Dr. Neal. After an examination, Dr. Neal informed him that surgery was imperative. This was unthinkable. Uncle Wilbert said, "But if I go to the hospital, who'll look after my cows?" Dr. Neal said quietly, "The same person who'll look after them if you don't." That got his attention and he submitted to the operation.

One summer, an insurance salesman was making his way around Pollard, trying to sell a policy here and there. When he got into his spiel about providing security for his family, Uncle Wilbert would have none of that, "When I die, I want everybody to be unhappy." (That is probably one of Victor's jokes that could apply to anyone.) But still and all, he wasn't about to spend any money on insurance.

They never attended church, but sometime during every revival Aunt Agnes enjoyed entertaining the preacher and the visiting evangelist. All the relatives were invited and the noon meal would rival any banquet served during the middle ages. Actually, (as Mr. Joe Reynolds would say) it really wasn't a noon meal, whoever heard tell of a Methodist preacher lettin' out church until at least one o'clock. But anyway, there would be country ham, fried chicken, baked hen and dressing, and pork tenderloin. Potatoes were cooked in every way imaginable and every vegetable known to man was served. Added to this were cakes, pies and ice cream. The table literally groaned with its bounty and the preachers, who had preached against every other imaginable sin, somehow ignored the sin of gluttony and unloosed another notch on their belt. Sometimes two notches.

After all the adults had their fill, the children were then told to come to the table. Yeah, I know, this sounds incredible to today's generation, when children are fed first, but we really didn't care, we were having so much fun playing hide n' go seek, we hardly noticed that were only chicken wings, gizzards and necks left. Yes, I said gizzards and necks.

Uncle Wilbert and Aunt Agnes had been married for forty-eight years and one morning he sat down to a breakfast of fried sugar cured shoulder, biscuits and eggs. Something about the biscuits was not to his liking and he started telling her about it. She said, "Well, I declare to my time, we've been married for forty-eight years and that's the first time you have ever said a word." He said, "Sy, that's the first time there's ever been anything wrong with them." Instead of being offended, she thought that was funny and told it all over Pollard. Actually, she told it at the store and it spread all over Pollard.

Aunt Agnes' parents, Kate and Orren Burton, lived in a very small house just up the road apiece. I called her Aunt Kate. When I was a child, I thought his name was spelled i-r-o-n, because everyone called him Arn, and that was also the way we pronounced iron.

Now Mr. Burton had a habit of preceding his every statement with the expression, "Pshaw!" In 1936, Roosevelt and Landon were running for president. On election night, most of the Kissin' Ridge residents were gathered at Uncle Wilbert's house to huddle around the radio and listen to the returns. Since most everyone in that section of Jessamine County voted the Republican ticket, there was a general feeling of unease as the announcer said, "The great state of Tennessee goes to Roosevelt!" or "The state of California goes to Roosevelt!" This continued until finally Mr. Burton had to re-assure his fellow Republicans that all was not lost. "Pshaw! jes wait til Spain comes in!"

When he was well up in his seventies, he had delusions of grandeur and started trying to fool around with a girl in her teens. One Saturday afternoon, he and some fellow loafers were seated around the stove at Garland's store. Among the crowd was Doc Vinson, who had only one eye (the other had been gouged out in a knife fight) and always had tobacco juice running down each corner of his mouth. Mr. Burton started bragging about his young girl friend and Doc looked at him with his one eye and said, "Arn, you have the head of a bull and the ass of a steer." I've always heard that even old rats still like cheese.

After he and his wife died, Aunt Agnes kept all their possessions in that little house just as they had left them. The house was locked and no one was ever allowed to set foot in the door. And of course, since I couldn't, and I knew I couldn't, I really, really wanted to see what was in that house. But I never did. I had heard that it was furnished with country antiques, and I knew for a fact that Aunt Kate owned one of those big pump organs. (What on earth would I have done with it if she had given it to me?) Aunt Agnes did give me four little pressed glass wine glasses. She had promised me a quilt made out of tobacco sacks, but I never saw that. That's another example of that generation's using everything. Cigarette tobacco was shredded, packed in little five-ounce drawstring bags and sold. This was poured into a three-inch long and one inch wide piece of tissue paper, and then rolled, and the edges licked, enabling them to stick together. This resulted into a fairly acceptable cigarette. As a matter of fact, it was very acceptable for no one could afford to buy ready mades. After all the tobacco was used, the cloth bag was ripped open, washed, dried and put aside until enough were accumulated to sew a quilt top.

I don't know if Odell ever asked Doreen to come back or not. My guess would be that he didn't for they had a stiff-necked pride that simply did not include begging or rejection. After she left, he started drinking and layin' out with disreputable women. He bought a trailer and parked it on some of their river bottomland. Then in 1953, their world came crashing down. Odell had gone home to his trailer one cold winter night and when he tried to light the gasoline heater, it exploded, igniting the trailer and burning its entire contents. Including Odell. Uncle Wilbert and Aunt Agnes were devastated. Aunt Agnes even lost all interest in work. For a while. Uncle Wilbert lived a few more years and after he died Aunt Agnes lived alone and although she lived pretty far back on Kissin' Ridge, she wasn't afraid of the devil himself. One of her neighbors owned a mule that knew how to escape from its own pasture and get into Aunt Agnes' cornfield. She got her shotgun and got the animal's attention--also his owners. Mother wrote that story to me when Robin was in the fifth grade and Robin thought that would be a good topic for an English assignment, and wrote a poem, My Aunt Agnes shot at a mule--That first line was all she could remember.

Mother and I usually visited her every time I went back to Pollard. She was always so happy to see us, and I was always welcome to any leftover blackberry cobbler or cold biscuits and pear preserves. "Why, honey, it's not much, but jest hep yourself, I wish Ida knowed you was comin, Ida had somethin good fer ye. And if you'll stay awhile, I'll fix somethin fit to eat."

All are buried in the Stinnett graveyard in Pollard. Their house is gone but the little house that was home to Aunt Kate and "Arn" Burton is one of only two or three that still stands on Kissin' Ridge. Doreen spent her remaining years in Lexington, where she suffered a stroke and remained in a nursing home until her death in 1995.

Mother and Daddy

They ran off (young people didn't elope back then) and were married in the year of 1917. She was 18; he was 17. In a letter to one of Aunt Vina's girls she wrote the following story of entering the life of matrimony. "Our Uncle taught at Pollard and every year, we'd go back into the eighth grade. He didn't have sense enough to have us go to Nicholasville and pass the test to enter High School. (The uncle was Uncle Alvin.) When I was seventeen, he retired and we had a new teacher who asked, "Dola, why are you still in the eighth grade, why aren't you in high school?" I went to town, passed the test and Poppy rented a room for me with three other young women. But I thought I would be too old when I graduated, so I, too, got married."

Calvin Comley outside of Oscar Comley's grocery

Clarence Huffines married them at a Baptist Church in Nicholasville. And that's all I know of their courtship and early-married life.

Dola Comley 1922

I don't even know where they spent the first few months of married life. However, I think it's safe to say that they didn't spend any time with Grandpa and Mommy Johns for she didn't like Daddy at all and for years, referred to him as that thing that Dola married.

It's fortunate that it really doesn't matter where they set up housekeeping for Victor doesn't know and neither do I. According to the custom of those days, the mother-to-be usually went to the maternal home place to give birth. I was born at Mommy Johns' house, which, at that time was located at the end of what is now called Johns' Lane.

My earliest memory was living in a little one-bedroom shack owned by Monroe Miller. And it really was a shack (But the last time I was in Pollard I noticed that it is still standing.) That was where Santa left the little pea organ. Next was the Owl Den, then Mother and Daddy moved in with great Grandpa Milford and that was when she began a lifetime taking care of old people.

Vic and I were speculating once about how great an influence Dad had been in our lives and all I could think of was, not very much. But when Vic was about 6 years old Dad decided that he was old enough to learn how to milk. It's been so long since I milked a cow that it's hard for me to explain the process, but here goes. At first the cow's bag is very full and the milk pours out with gentle pulling pressure on the teat. One uses both hands. Then comes the second part which is called stripping and requires more pressure and stronger pulling. For about a week, Dad came by and stripped the cow for him. Then one evening he walked right on by and Vic said, "Aren't you going to strip the cow for me?" And Dad replied, "It's time you learned to strip your own cow." That was almost the name of this book. "You got to learn to strip your own cow."

Dad could do most anything; he was a good carpenter, he operated a gristmill and there was nothing on the farm that he couldn't do. But his love of alcohol and driving to Lexington or the mountains interfered with steady work on the farm. Of course, there were certain things required of him - such as working in tobacco. When it was ready to cut it was just like anything else on a farm. It had to be done then and no waiting. He would come in from the tobacco patch and immediately start taking a bath. If I happened to be around, it was "Gwen, go somewhere else, I'm taking a bath." You wouldn't think he could take a bath from a small pan but that's how we all bathed. I think Dad was one of the cleanest men I have ever known. That's because his mother (maw) was a Fain. All of the Fains were notoriously fastidious and usually the ones who married them were the same by the process of osmosis. (With the exception of my mother who was a very clean cook, but the rest of the house was always messy. Although she never had any place to store anything.) Great Uncle Irey's wife, Aunt

Annie was a Reynolds but Uncle Irey was a Fain and when I went across the road to their house to play with Betty, I felt that I should take a bath before I went in and I wouldn't have picked my nose for any amount of money.

I've always said that Dad loved his grandchildren more than he did his own children. When we visited with our children, he always put silver dollars under their pillows at night. He told Laura and Missy that every time it rained in Pollard, arrow heads were washed up on one of the hillsides and just laying there for anyone who wished to pick them up. He happened to have a collection, and after a good hard rain he hurried out to scatter a few. What fun they had discovering those Indian artifacts.

He and Garland often went on scouting trips to the mountains. By scouting, I mean they were looking for anything they could buy and re sell. And Dad and Willie True often brought a truck load of produce to Nicholasville, parked it on the street and usually sold everything they had. But one Saturday, they had a bushel of pears that simply wasn't moving. Dad took all the bigger pears out, put the smaller ones in the bottom of the basket then laid the big ones on top and raised the price and sold the whole basket. His first cousin, Oscar Comley owned a grocery store and busy Saturdays would occasionally find Dad in the store with a white apron on cutting meat. As I said, he could do anything.

One Saturday, he had come into town early in the morning. He worked for Oscar a few hours and then started drinking. When he was ready to go home, he looked for his truck and found it loaded with loafers. He looked at them and said anybody who's not going to Pollard, get off. He got in the truck, started backing up and ran smack dab into a light pole by Bill Stott's Saloon. It was said that light pole bonged for ten minutes. And on the way home, he almost ran into the creek from the Mt. Lebanon Bridge. Harrison Hurt almost swallowed his chaw.

When he and Mother were in their early forties, both went to Irvin and had Uncle Henry pull all their teeth. They had to wait a few weeks while their gums healed before new dentures were made. He had a great time making faces and laughing at her. Wonder what "the other woman" thought about that?

Every summer Dad hauled used mayonnaise jars from Lexington and unloaded them in the front yard where a big table was set up under a shade tree. We filled a galvanized washtub with warm soapy water, and with the aid of a small mop always had a few dozen clean jars, which we sold for twenty-five cents a dozen. By "we" I mean Victor and me. Mother was usually too busy canning and preserving summer produce and when she wasn't doing that, she was sewing. She made all of her clothes and most all of mine. She could alter a coat or jacket to fit perfectly. She was a much better seamstress than I ever thought of being. Occasionally, she might bring me a "ready made" dress from Lexington and during the wintertime when she was working in Lexington at the R.J. Reynolds tobacco company she almost always brought me a book of paper dolls, or a new box of "colors." I loved coloring in a new coloring book and nothing pleased me more than owning a brand spanking new box of colors. They smelled as good as they looked.

Those years of working in Lexington were a trial to her as well as a means of earning money. By trial, I mean Dad was conveniently near 'the other woman'. But close proximity meant little to him. He probably enjoyed driving the 12 mile trip from Pollard to Lexington. I think he probably felt that a car or truck was a part of him. He was a heavy smoker and I can see him now with a cigarette in the corner of his mouth occasionally being transferred to the other corner by his tongue. When he was about 62, he was stricken with a severe heart attack. Since Mother had never learned to drive, he had no other recourse except to drive himself to a doctor in Nicholasville. From there on to a Lexington hospital where he remained for two weeks then sent home to recover. However, recovery was not to be. He started having other pains and losing weight. More tests found pancreatic cancer. He was firmly convinced that he could beat this until during a trip to his doctor, he was dismayed at the amount of weight he had lost. There was no treatment or cure. We took the children often but after a short visit, I had to take them out to Aunt Dallas' to play. Once when we were there, I walked in the house and Mother was in the bedroom where Dad was lying in bed and I heard her trying to teach him to pray. He was repeating after her, "Now I lay me down to sleep." I felt as intrusive as if I had walked in on them having sex. (I wonder if she thought he "made it.") He became so incapacitated that Mother needed help. She decided to try a nursing home in Nicholasville, but as soon as she walked in the door she was assailed by an odor and out she walked, saying "If it takes every penny I have he'll go back to the hospital." She called Vic, and Geraldine told her to bring him to their house. He died there about 5 days later. He is buried in Nicholasville in Maplelawn cemetery.

Prior to his death she had bought a house in Nicholasville practically next door to Uncle Herbert and Aunt Mayme. (Dad didn't want her living in the country by herself.) It was too large for one person so she had a kitchen and bathroom added to one half and rented it to Lulu Crutchfield until she died and then to Ethel Burton (or as Beth would say "Effel") I think she probably worked harder there than she did in the country. She started keeping children for working mothers, she baby sat at night and worked in Herbert's garden, canned tomatoes and beans, cured hams and although she hated to cook, found herself frying chickens for her friend, Jean Nickelson because "Mrs. Comley, you fry the best chicken I've ever tasted." She also cooked pinto beans for Vic's family, and for Joy and Bill when they lived in Lexington. And for good measure, she fried a few dried apple pies. Her talent for sewing also served her well for she let it be known that she could remodel a coat, shorten a skirt or work buttonholes. And all the while, she was saving money. She had learned the art of frugality from the master, her mother. As soon as she saved enough for a c.d. she'd go to the bank and buy one or else get Vic do her banking for her. He'd always say, "This is $500. for me and $500 for Gwen." and she thought that was funny. She always hid her deposit slips and bank certificates because she thought Lulu or 'Effel' would come in and look at them while she was working and she didn't want anyone else to know anything about her finances.

I think she enjoyed living in town although she never felt comfortable in city churches. After a while, she started going back to Mt. Beulah where she knew everyone and occasionally was asked to play the piano as well as teach a Sunday school class. Fortunately Pansy Hurt had remained a member of Mt. Beulah and was happy to have a passenger.

She never saw a movie, never drove a car, never had a drink of alcohol, never played any kind of cards and never wore a pants suit. "Wearing pants was a sin." Dad saw lots of movies, lived in a car or truck, and had lots of alcohol.

She had severe osteoporosis and was in constant back pain. Three untreated fractures only exacerbated the problem. Once she fell while climbing on a couch trying to align a window curtain. Another fracture occurred while helping Herbert cure hams. Not only did she have osteoporosis, she was also plagued with stomach problems. She wrote to Aunt Vina that she was afraid to go to a doctor because she thought she had cancer. Necessity finally drove her to seeing a physician who ordered tests from which it was discovered that she had severe high blood pressure. Medication was prescribed and B/P was somewhat controlled.

Dola Comley and Victor - 1920

She also formed personal friendships. Martha Shipp was a young neighbor who came over every Saturday and rolled her hair. Jean Nicholson often took her to Lexington. One of her "children" was Ann Daugherty's grandchild so Ann's mother often called to take them to McDonald's for a burger.

She even joined a home makers club and especially enjoyed the Christmas parties. They could have been the original re-gifters. Two or three wash cloths or kitchen towels were unwrapped, exclaimed over then carefully folded and passed on to someone else at a Sunday school party the next year.

Aunt Mayme always had a small tree decorated and of course she cooked a big dinner and presents were opened. Herbert was a great one for handing over a five dollar bill. They gathered all the leftovers plus a big bag of apples, oranges and candy and made a trip to Pollard to share with Roland and Clay.

When she was 86 and was suffering a weight loss, she was diagnosed with colon cancer.

Surgery was scheduled but she died two days before - Martha Shipp was with her because she was kind enough to think she was too sick to be alone. She refused to eat, just lay down on the couch and died a peaceful death. Vic thinks she willed herself to die because she didn't want doctors and hospitals to get any more of her money. I don't agree with him. I think she willed herself to die (if a person can do such) because she was so afraid of the surgery. She told me she was so afraid she would have to wear colostomy bag and that was all she could think of. She is buried beside Dad in Maple Lawn Cemetery.

* * * * * * *

In writing this I have come to the conclusion that there is enough material in every family to write its own book. Stories, secrets, tragedies. And mysteries passed down from one generation to the other.

I could not possibly have written everything in Stringer's life in one small chapter. There's the heartbreaking loss of his little Mary Ruth, an unheard of thing such as divorce, another marriage to Gertrude ended in her death at the tender age of twenty, all the stories about him and Gin. That relationship started with the watermelon episode and progressed to the sorghum cake story. Stringer was never full in his entire life and once asked Mabel, who was a marvelous cook if she would make him a sorghum cake. She was happy to do so and took him a mouth watering three-layer cake with "karmal" icing. He didn't get a bite of it for that happened to be one the times when Gin was mad at him and she took the cake to the back door and threw it down the holler. So there we have the stories, the tragedies, the secrets (or he thought it was a secret when he was layin' out with her) and the mysterious death of his young wife, Gertrude. And since Mabel was kind enough to share her sorghum cake recipe, I think it deserves a place in this story.

Mabel's sorghum cake

1 cup sorghum
1 cup white sugar
1 cup buttermilk
1 teaspoon soda
2 cups flour
1 tablespoon baking powder
2 eggs
2 sticks margarine

and one teaspoon each of vanilla, cinnamon, allspice and ginger. And like all good old cooks who bake by "feel" she gave no directions, but I'm going to test this before passing it on. (But I never did get around to this and probably won't.)

Then there's the true story of a first cousin who spent 15 years in the state penitentiary at Eddyville for a crime he did not commit. His son accidentally shot and killed a man and my cousin took the rap, so to speak. There was also a tragic death of a baby boy in that family. And from early on the oldest son was plagued with heart trouble; also marital problems for his wife owned the farm where they lived, and she more or less kicked him out. Uncle Herbert was good enough to let him live in one of his little houses and even paid his doctor bills and bought his medicine.

Then the good Lord knows the Davis family stories could have been serialized and sold like the Harry Potter books. Divorces alone would have filled one volume and Gene's layin' out another and the devotion Ruth and Esther had for each other would have been number three.

Epilogue

POLLARD—home-memories-nostalgia-Grandparents-aunts-uncles-cousins-great aunts and uncles-second cousins...

Thomas Wolfe said, "You can't go home again" Well, he was wrong. Often at night before sleep overtakes me I start from the little house on the corner past the store, go past Mr. Joe Reynolds' where their little bob-tailed dog rushes down to the fence, one end barking furiously to impress him, the other end wagging at me and hoping for a pat-nod Hidy to him-hurry on by the Reynolds graveyard (might see a haint) - walk on past the little shack that Monroe owned then past his house and on the left is Paschal's barn, then his and Francis' house where she walks out with a sack of green beans for me to take to Granny then on up a slight hill with Granny Bea's house on the right- wave at her as she sits out on her porch and the empty school house on the left past her barn then the church and down a hill until I see Mommy Johns' house. I don't stop because Esther had told me they were going to can tomatoes and I sure didn't want to wash canning jars. I arrive at the gap in the hedge row and my bare feet can STILL feel the wash outs before going up through the old orchard to Granny's and Grandads. I walk in through the back porch and look first to see what she has cooked and what is left over because there is always something good on the stove. But first I have to go get a bucket of cold water then I usually eat a plate of green beans and a ros'near and then some black berry cobbler. So don't tell me you can't go home again - I guess Pollard's not such a long way off after all!

Made in the USA
Lexington, KY
01 September 2016